ALL THINGS NEW

A STUDY ON 2 CORINTHIANS
FOR TEEN GIRLS

KELLY MINTER

LifeWay Press® / Nashville, Tennessee

Published by LifeWay Press®

©2016 Kelly Minter

Reprinted Mar. 2017, July 2017

Author's literary agent is D.C. Jacobson & Associates LLC, an Author Management Company, www.dcjacobson.com.

ISBN: 978-1-4300-5993-6

Item 005787455

Dewey Decimal Classification Number: 248.83

Subject Heading: RELIGION/ Christian Ministry/ Youth

Printed in the United States of America

Student Ministry Publishing
LifeWay Resources
One LifeWay Plaza
Nashville, Tennessee 37234-0144

We believe that the Bible has God for its author; salvation for its end; and truth, without any mixture of error, for its matter and that all Scripture is totally true and trustworthy. To review LifeWay's doctrinal guideline, please visit www.lifeway.com/doctrinalguideline.

TABLE OF CONTENTS

For more information
on the work
JUSTICE AND MERCY
INTERNATIONAL
is doing around the
world, check out
justiceandmercy.org.

KELLY MINTER IS AN AUTHOR, SPEAKER, AND SONGWRITER. SHE IS PASSIONATE ABOUT WOMEN DISCOVERING JESUS THROUGH THE PAGES OF SCRIPTURE, SO WHETHER IT'S THROUGH STUDY, SONG, OR THE SPOKEN WORD, KELLY'S DESIRE IS TO AUTHENTICALLY EXPRESS CHRIST TO THE WOMEN AND GIRLS OF THIS GENERATION. SHE HAS FOUND DEEP HOPE AND HEALING THROUGH THE BIBLE'S TRUTHS, MAKING HER MESSAGE PERSONAL AND RELATIONAL.

No Other Gods, the first installment of The Living Room Series, helps women unveil the false gods in their lives for the ultimate purpose of discovering freedom in the one, true God. *Ruth: Loss, Love & Legacy* follows the redemptive story of Ruth, displaying God's providence and purpose even in the most trying circumstances. *Nehemiah: A Heart That Can Break* is an unforgettable journey into the missional heart of God. *What Love Is: The Letters of 1, 2, 3 John* look at the words of the Beloved Disciple regarding life in Christ. All studies are presented in the same Living Room Series format (studies can be done in any order). Kelly also released her first memoir, *Wherever The River Runs: How A Forgotten People Renewed My Hope In The Gospel*, about her life-changing journeys to the Amazon jungle.

Kelly writes extensively and speaks at women's conferences and events around the country. She has her own event called Cultivate: A Women's Gathering Around The Word. This biblically based and stylistically simple event is for women of all ages. Kelly also partners closely with Justice and Mercy International, an organization that cares for the vulnerable and forgotten in the Amazon and Moldova. Kelly's music includes *Loss, Love & Legacy*, which complements her Ruth study, and the worshipful *Finer Day,* and *Hymns & Hallelujahs*. To view more about Kelly's studies, books, music, and calendar, visit *www.kellyminter.com.*

ABOUT THE STUDY

This eight-session resource will guide girls through the Letter of 2 Corinthians. They will complete five days of homework each week and then you will meet to discuss it as a group. The final session includes a Leader Guide that will serve as a helpful tool as you walk through this study with a group of girls.

Our prayer is that the girls in your group will learn about the church at Corinth and how Paul ministered to them, but more importantly, that they will be challenged to grow and live in light of 2 Corinthians. Girls will see how Christ can use our weaknesses for His glory and gain a firsthand understanding of how if anyone is in Christ, he or she is a new creation.

꧁ A **NOTE** FROM **KELLY** ꧂

If you'd asked me at the beginning of writing this study why I wanted to spend a year in 2 Corinthians, I would have pointed to all those wonderful passages like the thorn in the flesh, Christ's power in our weakness, the heavenly bodies we will one day receive, God's comfort in suffering, and a whole two chapters on generosity and the poor. These passages worked as anchors for my soul during the calm and storms of life. I grew up on the truth of these beloved texts.

One of the earliest spiritual metaphors I learned was from 2 Corinthians, where Paul talked about carrying the treasures of knowing Jesus as if in fragile jars of clay. This has been especially meaningful to me, because I've always longed to be a more steadfast Christian—someone who has it together. But, honestly? I still don't have it together. I simply can't get away from this. But after meditating on Paul's words, I'm reminded I don't have to: "For when I am weak, then I am strong" (2 Cor. 12:10b).

Maybe more than anything, it is the weakness and honesty with which Paul wrote that has moved me. Scholars have often described 2 Corinthians as Paul's most personal letter, and this may be one of the reasons I never tire of returning to its pages. It is a passionate, pleading, even provocative letter at times, where Paul exposed his outstretched heart to a community of somewhat inconsistent believers who frankly didn't seem to care for him as much as he cared for them. Paul's heartbreak over their failures and enthusiasm over their restoration remind us of how relational the ministry of the gospel is. I just don't ever want to forget that if I lose my heart for people, then I've lost the purpose of ministry.

Speaking of ministry, if your only experience with the Christian faith has been rule-bound and oppressive, well then, might I invite you to the new covenant version? Paul spent valuable ink explaining that, since the coming of Christ, the way we minister to others is more gracious, humble, powerful, Spirit-filled, life-giving, and freeing than we ever imagined. He seemed to sum the whole thing up in one word: glorious.

So that is how I began—eager to write about all the things I knew I loved about 2 Corinthians. Yet, after having immersed myself in the text, I discovered it was all the passages less familiar to me that have so surprised and changed me. My hope is that you too might rediscover a letter you thought you already knew. And if you've never done a Bible study before, all the more reason for you to explore its pages. One of the great anchors of Paul's letter is that Christianity isn't for the religious elite—I promise, the Corinthians will do a great job of backing this up. I warmly invite you, mature believer or new explorer, on a journey through this ancient letter.

The old has passed away, behold the new has come.

HOW TO USE

Review & Begin
As you prepare each week, spend time in prayer. Then, review the homework from the previous session, and highlight anything noteworthy to share with the girls in your group. For the first session, we ask for you to review the Session 1 introduction, found on pages 9-11. After reading the introduction, take notes as you skim the Group Guide. Then, begin the five days of homework.

Homework Instructions
If you have a busy week, you might need to double-up and complete two days to get ahead. Scripture should be the main focus, so if girls are pressed for time, suggest they first read through the passage of Scripture listed for that session. Within the homework, there are questions based on the Scripture passage, as well as application questions which are labeled Personal Reflection and Personal Response. Record your responses in the book or in your own journal.

Group Guide Instructions
The two-page Group Guide is included after each session's introduction. It is designed and formatted as a tool to review the homework from the previous session and introduce the current session and homework for the week to come.

There will be several things girls will be asked to answer or journal about throughout the study. Be creative with this and allow them to express their own forms of creativity, whether that be through drawing or Scripture doodling. You will want to consider providing paper, colored pencils and pens, or other craft supplies.

Encourage girls to bring a journal of their own where they can write or draw their thoughts, ideas, and responses to Scripture. The margins of this book are also designed to give girls a space to answer questions and record their thoughts as they journey through the Letter of 2 Corinthians.

THE CHURCH IN A CITY

2 Corinthians 1:1–2:11

My friend Kelly is a singer/songwriter growing up in the thick of country music land. I'd asked Kelly to be part of a group that would work through the *All Things New* homework and provide feedback. She obliged and provided great insight.

At the end of our study, Kelly asked if we could meet to discuss 2 Corinthians. We jotted a date on the calendar because you don't have to ask me twice to meet you for coffee, conversation, and Corinthians. That's almost too much goodness for one morning.

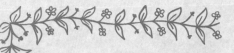

In some ways, Kelly's mulling over 2 Corinthians yielded more revelation than questions. She'd become acquainted with the problems in Corinth—its lust for power, zeal for social status, affinity for pleasure, vulnerability to deception so similar to our own—and noticed Paul's message went against the current, dodging the culture and all of its values as they rushed past him downstream. Paul was headed to a different destination. He was on mission for Jesus. And when your mission is different from the world's, you'll find yourself maneuvering through the oncoming crowds.

"Everything is the opposite!" Kelly said, lifting her tea in the air. "I mean everything Paul says, is like, the exact opposite of what we're told we're supposed to live for." (Toss in the flash and fame of the music industry, and the opposites become polar.)

I knew what Kelly meant. After nearly a year in this letter, I too felt the inescapable tension between Paul's life and the life of ease and comfort. But don't get all squirmy on me. Paul champions the paradoxical life of a believer with unfathomable love. Now that we've got that straight, here are just a few of the opposites:

- Our celebrity industry prizes youth, beauty, and in many ways perfection, while Paul writes about boasting in our weaknesses so Christ can receive the glory.

- We're taught to have razor-sharp competence so we can claw our way to the top of our schools and communities, but Paul says our competence makes us better ministers.

- When someone offends us, we close off our hearts so as not to be invaded again. However, when the church bruised Paul, he returned with his heart open wide.

- When we finally get a little authority handed to us we think it's meant for bossing everyone around, but could it be our authority is for building people up and working for their joy? Paul thought so.

Wow!

- Our instincts tell us to hang onto our money so we can spend it on ourselves and have plenty for later, while Paul points to a poor church in Macedonia that wanted to give its money away because they saw it not as a duty but, get this, a privilege.

No doubt Kelly was onto something. The Christian life is indeed one of paradox. What Jesus holds dear is opposite of what we naturally tend to cling to. What struck me was that Kelly's revelation didn't leave her discouraged, but relieved. She found Paul's message freeing. She was happy to know she could still write songs, but she no longer had to perform for the ever-changing approval of others. She doesn't need to concern herself with keeping in step with the latest trends when being commended by Jesus is the highest praise—all that satisfies. And it won't matter if her life lands her on the grandest stage in NYC or in a small country church; however the Lord wants to use her gift will be her joy. And whomever the Lord brings across her path will be her ministry. Yep, 2 Corinthians is a letter of opposites. It's a letter about the adventurous faith of hanging all of our hope on God. It's about an abiding peace at the ocean floor of our souls that oddly doesn't roll in after a manicure or upon receiving acceptance to an Ivy League college. Instead of having to earn or buy our peace, peace comes when our sins are no longer counted against us because God sent His Son, Jesus, into the world to take our sins upon Himself. Paul called this reconciliation.

As you work your way through 2 Corinthians, consider the opposites. Note the way Paul unconditionally loved the Corinthians, what he rejoiced in, who he trusted, and what he called home. Then, think about what the world loves, celebrates, hopes in, and rests its head on when life is tough. As you consider the striking differences, never forget you've been empowered to live beautifully and unashamedly set apart because, since Jesus' death and resurrection, the old has gone, and the new has come. And last time I checked, old and new are as opposite as they come.

Group Guide (Week 1)

Welcome to the first group session for *All Things New*! This time will be more of a general introduction to the study and the Letter of 2 Corinthians, as well as a time for you to get to know those in your group. There are so many rich truths for us to explore in 2 Corinthians, so let's dive in!

Prepare

Read the introduction on the previous three pages prior to your group's first meeting. Circle, highlight, or underline anything that sticks out to you in the introduction or in the passage of Scripture. Pray that God would use this study to draw you closer to Himself and to help you to hide His Word in your heart.

Review & Discuss

Review the introduction again together as a group, and then discuss the following questions.

What do you hope to gain from this study and from being a part of this group?

What do you know about Corinth or the Letter of 2 Corinthians?

Consider the diverse culture of your school or community. Discuss this as a group, as well as what the diverse culture of Corinth may have been like.

According to Paul, what is *reconciliation* (2 Cor. 5:18-19)? Explain this in your own words.

List some opposites or oxymorons that come to mind (jumbo shrimp, short wait, tiny elephant, true myth, worthless gold, etc.).

What were some of the opposites in Paul's life when compared with a life of ease? How did these things set Paul apart as a follower of Christ?

In what ways is your <u>life set apart for Christ</u>? What are some practical things you can do this week to live for Him in your home and at school?

Jot down one thing you have learned so far, either from the introduction or from these questions and your group's discussion. Also record one question you have.

Journal

Think about your expectations for what you would like to gain from this study and jot them down. Journal your goals and what time commitment you are making to be a part of a group as you complete the next seven weeks of this study.

Take Action

Complete the following five days of homework before the next group meeting. Take notes and highlight anything that you might want to share with the group during the next time you meet.

• **Memorize:** 2 Corinthians 1:5-6

DAY 1
A Seemingly Unlikely Place for a Church *(2 Cor. 1:1-2)*

Whenever I visit a city I've never been to before I research it online. Something about seeing the actual landscape of a place, eating at its restaurants, and strolling its well-known streets makes me want to better understand its history and happenings. Of course, I also want to know what stars live there. The same is true when I start studying a book of the Bible. Learning about context and historical placement is vital to gaining a more accurate understanding of the book at hand.

Before we dive into 2 Corinthians, let's set the stage. Paul first visited Corinth and established the church there in A.D. 50-51. We learn from 1 Corinthians 5:9 that he wrote an instructive letter that is now lost. After hearing about significant problems in the church, Paul wrote the letter we know as 1 Corinthians around A.D. 53/54. After that letter he wrote what is referred to as the "sorrowful letter," also presumed to be lost. This brings us to 2 Corinthians, which Paul wrote in response to hearing that the church had experienced a few victories along with some failures that needed to be addressed. We'll get to know more about these issues in the days ahead, issues that will feel surprisingly familiar to us 2,000 years later.

CORINTHIAN CHRONOLOGY:

AD 50-51
Paul establishes church in Corinth

AD 52
Writes instructive letter (1 Cor. 5:9); this letter is lost

AD 53-54
Writes 1 Corinthians.

AD 54
Makes "sorrowful visit" to Corinth.

AD 54
Writes "painful letter" (2 Cor. 2:3-4); this letter is lost

AD 54
Writes 2 Corinthians

AD 56
Makes final visit to Corinth

Let's read 2 Corinthians 1:1-2 as we begin this journey together.

Paul was writing to the church at Corinth. Think about the most culturally electric city you've ever visited. You may have taken in a play or a movie, or doused your senses with ancient paintings or relics while strolling through museums. If you're like my sister, Katie, you spotted a celebrity—she finds them everywhere she goes. Bright lights and garish signs, taxi horns and symphonies, violence and class, rich and poor and everyone in between, trying to find their way in this place we've known since nearly the beginning of time: the city.

You could make the argument that first century Corinth was the citiest of cities.

When Paul arrived, Corinth was at the pinnacle of its development. A commercial epicenter of Southern Greece, perched on an isthmus (think Seattle and Google it for a photo) that brimmed with tourists and trade due to its two harbors, Lechaeum and Cenchreae. Corinth was thriving, wealthy, and steeped in a blend of Roman and Greek culture. The ancient city of Corinth boasted everything you could ever want. But, as we know, having access to everything we could ever want doesn't always end up being what we thought we wanted.

The richness of Corinth's culture had its downsides, as do our own modern day cities: prostitution, slavery, foreign pagan practices, poverty, and sexual perversion of all kinds. False gods were everywhere. The temple of Aphrodite, the Greek goddess of love and life, was a central shrine in Corinth. As one scholar put it, Corinth was the "Vanity Fair" of Rome.[1]

Turn to Acts 18:1-11 and read about Paul's first visit to Corinth. We'll gather some basic facts, so think from the perspective of a reporter.

What couple did Paul live with? What country did they move from?

What type of work did Paul initially do to support himself?
    Cut Hair
    Fish
    Make Tents
    All of the above

What two people groups did he teach in the synagogues?

One night the Lord spoke to Paul in a vision: "Do not be afraid; keep on speaking, do not be silent. For I am with you, and no one is going to attack and harm you, because I have many people in this city."
Acts 18:9-10

According to verse 8, what happened to many of the Corinthians Paul taught?

In Acts 18:9-10, where did the Lord tell Paul He had many people?

This is a comforting and encouraging word for wherever we find ourselves living.

If the gospel of Jesus transformed Corinth's prostitutes, religious, wealthy, pagans, farmers, merchants, athletes, slaves, and synagogue leaders (like the one you just read about in Acts 18), then the good news of Jesus Christ can transform the people of our cities today. Though I'm tempted at times to think that God's people are only found in religious settings, God had His people in Corinth—in the city—just like God has you and me in the cultural settings we live in.\

Read the opening lines of 1 Corinthians 1:1-2. Paul gave an additional description of the believers in Corinth.

If he were writing to a group of monks or nuns you might think, *okay, they have a good shot at this holiness, sanctification, and purity thing*. But people in the middle of a place like Corinth, with no prior history of Christianity, being seen in God's eyes as holy? (See margin for definition.) Second Corinthians reminds us that God's church shines most brightly in the darkness rather than in already lit sanctuaries.

Personal Reflection: What about your culture makes it difficult for you to live a holy life?

In the days ahead we'll see how Paul pursued God's people with unrivaled fervor. They were a struggling church, filled with individuals who had bought into the trends and passions of the environment they lived in. I can relate to this. If I'm not alert and aware, I can easily slip into accepting the popular beliefs of the day.

We'll dig much deeper into Scripture in the coming days, but today I want you to understand the context for what we'll be studying. I'm excited to journey with you as we examine together what some have called Paul's most personal letter.

Girls, you are not alone. I think Paul said it best in his opening words, we're in this "together with all the saints."

Hagiazo: to make holy, (i.e. ceremonially) purify or consecrate; hallow, be holy, sanctify[2]

DAY 2
The God of All Comfort *(2 Cor. 1:3-11)*

I once held the idea that if I followed the principles laid out for me in Scripture, if I loved God and made wise, biblical choices, then I would be blessed with some version of a really good life, void of <u>heartbreak or catastrophe.</u> Somewhere deep down I knew that following God didn't guarantee this premium package, this safeness—I'd seen godly people suffer. But I also felt that if I did my part, then God would be obligated to do His: build me the kind of life we covet here in America and protect me from pain. This seemed like a reasonable expectation.

For the record, I do believe obedience yields blessing and that God delights in giving us gifts, often in response to our following Him. But what I missed during all those years of pining after what made me feel good, and attempting to protect myself from whatever I feared "coming upon me" (in the words of Job), was really quite simple: Suffering is part of the blessing.

The thought of suffering shouldn't frighten us because God is especially present in our suffering, but we also shouldn't set out for a life of pain or martyrdom in Jesus' name. We've been around the woe-is-me people, dressed in their Forever 21 sackcloth, who make us want to roll our eyes in frustration. Bottom line, we shouldn't fear suffering, but we don't need to be searching for it either.

Read 2 Corinthians 1:3-11.

Paul praised God as the Father of _____ **and the God of all** _____ **(v. 3).**

You've already noted that Paul opened his letter to the Corinthians by addressing two of God's characteristics that meet us in our afflictions (trouble or tribulations). Notice the impact of Paul's phrase in verse 3, "Father of compassion." Paul didn't say that God is a merciful Father, though He is, rather Paul said He's the Father of compassion. This is a shift for the person who sees God as someone who occasionally taps into His kind side.

Let's consider the original language of the word *mercies (compassion)*. The Greek word for mercies is *oiktirmos* and is used only five times in the New Testament. This word means "bowels in which compassion resides, a heart of compassion, emotions, longings, manifestations of pity,"[3] or "the inward parts."[4] When we look at the definition of this word we get a strong sense of feeling. According to Scripture, I want you to hear today what the Lord feels for you.

Flip back to 2 Corinthians 1:5. In this passage Paul stated that Christ's sufferings overflow into our lives. What do you think this means?

When Paul talks about the sufferings of Christ spilling over into our lives, part of what I think he was talking about is that believers will suffer certain things because they are living in obedience to Christ. Many Christians are suffering severe persecution around the world while others are mocked in lesser, but still painful, ways for their faith. Maybe you were passed over for an office in a club, endured ridicule from friends, or were betrayed or abandoned because of your belief in Jesus. When we suffer, we're uniquely associating with Jesus. Paul realized there is a certain fellowship that we have with Jesus during times of suffering, a distinct way that we identify with Him.

Personal Reflection: How have you become more deeply acquainted with Jesus as a result of sharing with Him in His sufferings?

I've yet to meet a person who enjoys suffering, but I've met many who've grown closer to Jesus during suffering. There are certain parts of Jesus you just can't know on a path of ease, and once you've tasted that closeness with Him, you won't trade it for the smooth course. In addition to experiencing a special fellowship with Jesus (Phil. 3:10), Paul revealed another reason suffering brings blessing.

Whenever Christ's sufferings overflow into our lives, what overflows out of us (v. 5)? This is so awesome to me.

In Brazil there's a natural phenomenon called *The Meeting of the Waters* where the Rio Negro and Rio Solimões meet. This meeting place forms what Brazilians consider as the official starting point of the Amazon River. The Rio Negro looks like a river of Coke; the Rio Solimões appears to be flowing with coffee and cream. When you sail on this part of the Amazon, you float down one grand body of water made up of two very distinct rivers. Even though the Rio Negro and Rio Solimões don't appear to mix for several miles, they are one. And as Christ's sufferings and comfort can also seem incongruent, you will never have one without the other—Christ's sufferings and His comfort flow together.

In verse 9, what reason did Paul give for having gone through these hardships?

According to verse 10, where did all of Paul's hope lie?

One of the most beautiful declarations in Scripture is found in verse 4. When we experience trials, it's often hard to see outside of our pain. But we find great purpose in our sufferings when we realize our experiences will serve as unique comforts to others going through similar pain.

If we want to be able to comfort others with the comfort we've received from God, then we need to be comfort-able. What I mean is that I've experienced times in my life when I didn't want to be comforted or didn't know how to be—when I was just plain mad. If we find ourselves in situations where we are unable to be comforted or encouraged, there is a problem. Receiving comfort requires humility before the Lord, open hands that say we need our Savior.

Personal Response: In what ways/areas do you need to be comforted? What's keeping you from pouring out your heart to the Lord and receiving His comfort today?

Paul was pushed beyond the end of himself—far beyond his ability to endure. I'm in no way claiming I've experienced sufferings at the same level as Paul's, but countless times I've come to the point when I realized I didn't have what it took to fix my situation. But far more importantly than simply coming to the end of myself, I came to God—the one who raises the dead.

As the rivers Negro and Solimões flow as one, Christ's suffering and His comfort run together in our lives, side by side. As Christians, we never have to suffer without Christ's comfort, and I believe there are certain comforts we will never know apart from His suffering. If you are going through a trial, maybe one far beyond your ability to endure, draw on God's comfort—the comfort that runs straight through the person of Jesus and into your life. He promises comfort in measure to your pain. And when you meet with God's consolation, you'll be eager to bind up the wounds of another person who experiences similar pain because God's comfort is overflowing in nature. You'll have more than enough comfort to share.

DAY 3
A Change of Plans *(2 Cor. 1:12-24)*

So, one of my mom's most common phrases in response to my badgering her about something I wanted to do was, "We'll see." It took me twenty years to realize this was code for, "The answer is 99% no way, kiddo," I was always hopeful. I use "We'll see" with my nieces and nephews all the time. It's a great way to remain honest, yet uncommitted, especially if you might need to change your plans.

As we go along, we'll discover that Paul was anything but a "we'll see" kind of guy. His yes was yes and his no was no, but this didn't mean Paul never had to change his plans. In today's reading, Paul explained to the Corinthians why he didn't visit them when he originally intended. We'll also get an idea about how the Corinthians felt about this.

Read 2 Corinthians 1:12-24.

If there's one thing about studying 2 Corinthians that's challenged me personally, it's that Paul didn't shy away from dealing with difficulty in relationships. We'll get into this further, but the Corinthians had some issues with Paul—his not showing up when he said he would being one of them. But before Paul jumped into an explanation of his actions, he first established his heart toward them.

> **Revisit verse 12. What three things characterized the actions of Paul and his friends toward the Corinthians? Circle them.**
>
> | | | | |
> |---|---|---|---|
> | Kindness | Holiness (purity) | Gentleness | Power |
> | Sincerity | Humility | Grace | Strength |

Before we move too far into the heart of this passage, let's take a look at where we are on the timeline (see p. 14) of Paul's relationship with the Corinthian church.

> **According to verses 15-16, what were Paul's initial travel plans?**

The church had not responded well to 1 Corinthians. Paul's ministry partner, Timothy, had visited the Corinthians after Paul wrote that letter and reported significant problems—moral issues, corrupted beliefs, and relational factions to name a few. As a result, Paul sailed from Ephesus to Corinth to deal with the Corinthians in person, which he referred to in 2 Corinthians 2:1-2 as a "sorrowful visit."

During this difficult visit, Paul probably told them that he'd see them again on his trip from Macedonia back to Judea.[5] However, when the Corinthians continued to attack him, it's reasonable to assume he made the decision to not return for a while. You can probably relate to trying to work out a difficult relationship, whether in person or through a letter. Paul had tried both and wasn't having much success.

Today's text reveals that the Corinthians questioned Paul's motives for not coming. Although he loved them dearly, a band of opponents stirred up the Corinthian church, casting doubt about the true and sincere nature of Paul's devotion. I personally cannot stand being misunderstood, especially in a situation where I've bent over backward, sacrificed, stood up, or gone out on a limb for someone. I'm not saying this happens to me often, but when it does, I wrestle with two basic decisions: First, do I trust the Lord with my reputation, resting in a clear conscience before Him (1:12)? Second, can I continue to love those who have accused me?

Wow!

Personal Reflection: What is your default reaction when you're misunderstood or falsely accused?

Paul wasn't into mixing his *yeses* and *noes*, saying one thing but doing another. According to verses 18-19, why was his ministry to the Corinthians straightforward and trustworthy?

It's usually not meant as a compliment when someone tells you you're being defensive about something. We may think the only godly response is to remain silent and never explain ourselves. (Prov. 9:8 says not to "rebuke a mocker.") However, sometimes explaining our actions is not only appropriate, but also vital to the relationship. So, how do you know if you should defend yourself or not? Here's a litmus test I use: If defending myself is motivated by self-protection and characterized by pride, anger, fear, or self-righteousness, it's most likely from my flesh. On the other hand, if defending myself is motivated by love for the other person and characterized by clarity, humility, kindness, and sincerity, it's from the Spirit. We'll note throughout this letter that Paul was clearly defending himself, not for self-defense's sake, but for the love of the Corinthians.

great advice

What reason did Paul give for not having gone to Corinth (v. 23)?

Whether we serve as leaders at our schools and churches, or even if we don't hold other positions of authority, we could solve a multitude of problems if we worked for the joy of those we oversee. *AMEN*

In other words, if we're motivated by power, significance, others' opinions, money, or self-worth, then our leadership is not based on God's love. The people we serve can tell if we're leading them out of self-interest or for their joy.

In a world that can feel so unsure, Paul reminds us the anchor of our souls is this: God is sure and faithful (v. 18). Do you see what he's saying? God is not careless. He doesn't trick us by mixing messages. He is faithful. We may know this, but have we allowed the faithfulness and trustworthiness of God to settle into our hearts? And do we believe everything that truly matters is "yes" in Jesus Christ? Fill in the following phrases based on what you've learned today.

Because God is faithful, He will _____.

Because God is faithful, I will _____.

DAY 4
Sincere and Straightforward *(2 Cor. 1:12-24)*

Today we will dig deeper into the text we studied yesterday. I had to camp out here a little longer because this text holds so much wisdom for us, especially we highly relational young women who can occasionally be passive-aggressive, insincere, or codependent— or is it just me? (It's probably just me.) First, let's revisit the word "sincerity" in verse 12. Remember how Paul explained to the Corinthians that postponing his trip came out of a sincere heart, not because Paul's heart was perfect, but because the sincere love he had for the Corinthians was from God—something he specifically wanted them to know.

I want you to see something really interesting about Paul's use of the word "sincerity" in an earlier letter.

> **Turn back to 1 Corinthians 5:6-8. What metaphor did Paul use to describe the difference between purity and sincerity versus malice and wickedness?**

The Feast of Unleavened Bread is a festival the Israelites celebrate in remembrance of their deliverance out of Egypt. Ridding their houses of yeast was symbolic of their purity before God. All these years later, Paul reminded the church in Corinth that a much more dangerous yeast needed to be removed—the one in their hearts. This leaven of malice and evil was spilling into conversations, spreading into relationships, and poisoning their community. As when yeast enters a batch of dough and spreads its effect throughout, so does the sin we allow to fester in our thoughts and hearts. Paul was urging them, and us, to rid ourselves of evil and live with sincerity! (This was way before the gluten-free muffin— Paul was so ahead of his time.)

Sincerity is somewhat of a lost quality in our time—it is overrun *authentic* by manipulation, shading the truth, passive-aggressive responses, lying, and flattery. How much richer could the body of Christ be if we were pure and sincere toward one another, as well as to those in the world?

> **Paul detailed more specifically what sincerity looks like. Revisit 2 Corinthians 1:17-20. What two, small, single-syllable words did Paul emphasize in this text?**

In verse 17, what did Paul say he did not do "in the same breath" (or simultaneously)?

What does it appear the Corinthians were accusing Paul of being?
   Wishy-washy
   Fickle
   Shady
   All of the above

We may not purposefully tell people yes when we really mean no, or say no when we really mean yes, but all of us have a way of doing exactly this in subtle ways. We say things like, "No really, I'm fine," while giving someone the silent treatment. We claim we've forgiven someone, but then punish that person by withholding friendship. Or maybe we make a commitment to something but carry it out annoyed—essentially saying yes with a huge no in our hearts. Or we do the opposite—we say no with our words while every other part of our lives is saying yes to what we should be resisting.

Personal Reflection: Are you in a situation where your yes is not really your yes, or your no is not really your no? If so, prayerfully commit to straightening out your yeses and noes in this situation.

If we stopped here we'd have a helpful lesson in integrity and forthrightness. But I'm so grateful Paul didn't stop here because today's study is about so much more than merely upping our integrity meter. Go with me here.

Who had Paul and his friends been preaching about to the Corinthians (v. 19)? The _____ of God, _____ _____.

Do you see that this is not merely a message about trying to do better, but is all about the person of Jesus? But Paul goes even further.

All the promises that God has made are _____ in Christ (v. 20).

The Christian faith is not merely about achieving moral standards for the sake of being really good people. Paul had already spent much of his life trying to be a good person by achieving a stellar Jewish education, being a member of the Pharisees, being trained by a top rabbi, and executing self-righteousness flawlessly. But he realized all of his "goodness" amounted to nothing but a dung heap. That's literally how he put it.

As Paul defended his actions to the Corinthians, his point was that being wishy-washy or untrustworthy toward them would go against the essence of the message that God is faithful. He cannot lie. He cannot go back on His Word. He made a covenant promise to redeem His children, and every promise included in that is "yes" in Jesus. If God is not fickle with his yeses and noes, well, then Paul shouldn't be either.

I wonder if one of the reasons we're not always sincere or straightforward in our relationships is because we're not grounded in the "yes" of Christ. I know I've waffled, flip-flopped, and gone back on my word at times because I wanted to make my life work the way I wanted it to. Sticking to a "yes" or "no" may have threatened that pursuit. But when I'm able to trust God's faithfulness, allowing that and His character to rule over my life, I don't have to be manipulative or insincere.

Personal Response: As we close today's study, what's been the most convicting part for you? If you can connect it to a specific phrase or verse from our text, jot down the phrase or verse alongside what you've learned.

Main point

"But whatever was to my profit I now consider loss for the sake of Christ. What is more, I consider everything a loss compared to the surpassing greatness of knowing Christ Jesus my Lord, for whose sake I have lost all things. I consider them rubbish, that I may gain Christ." (Phil. 3:7–8)

DAY 5
Not to be Outwitted *(2 Cor. 2:1-11)*

In the first part of today's reading, we'll encounter a situation every one of us has faced: Disappointing people we depend on to make us happy. In other words, when we have to confront a friend we love and enjoy—someone we like to go to Starbucks with—and we know this confrontation will make our friend upset or mad, then who will we have to text and grab a frappé with? We've all dealt with this dilemma, which is one of the reasons I love the way Paul addressed the scenario in 2 Corinthians.

Read 2 Corinthians 2:1-4.

Summarize why Paul decided to stay in Ephesus.

For what specific purpose did Paul say he wrote this letter (v. 4)?

One of the reasons we avoid confronting sin in another person's life is that we've made happiness the chief goal of our relationships— our own or the other person's. But true love shoots for holiness, which is not, as we may fear, stiff or boring. Holiness is the foundation on which thriving relationships find their footing. Whatever sin Paul addressed in the lives of the Corinthians—sin that was eating them alive (some of which we'll find out in more detail)—he wasn't confronting them to hurt them but to let them know how deeply he cared! Perhaps one of the greatest ways we fail to love people is when we say or do nothing while they struggle, all because we don't want to stir things up.

According to verse 4, Paul did not write for the sake of causing _____.

Paul wrote to express his love. In the original language, Paul grammatically positioned the word *love* in a way the Corinthians couldn't miss. Not only did he emphasize how greatly he loved them, but he also wanted them to know it. Who hasn't felt this way about someone we've so desperately wanted to see healed, restored, or delivered? We love them but they may not know it, and we want them to know it.

You may have someone in your life you long to see free from sin. I wonder if this person interprets your desire as being motivated by something other than love? Even if you've approached them in humility, mercy and kindness, do you think they view you as a killjoy or holier-than-thou? Explain.

Personal Response: Pause and pray that this loved one will receive your concern and correction as love.

Read 2 Corinthians 2:5-11.

Before we get into the details of who this person might be, whom did he grieve and cause pain (v. 5)?

Why did Paul advise the church to forgive and _____ him (v. 7)? Fill in the blank and respond.

Some believe this offender is the man Paul wrote about in 1 Corinthians 5:1-5 who had committed incest. Other scholars disagree because the details don't seem to match. What we do know is that this specific person had attacked Paul personally, which in turn affected the whole church community. This man's offense seems to be the focal point of a lot of the heartbreak Paul experienced with the Corinthians. Whatever the man's offense, it was significant.

In response to Paul's directive, the Corinthian church had taken some sort of disciplinary action toward this man. They probably removed the man from fellowship for a time, but in this passage Paul called for his restoration. The discipline had been effective and it was time to restore him to the community.

Personal Response: You've already noted that Paul urged the church to forgive and comfort this person. In verse 8 Paul told them to reaffirm their love for this man. What do you think this reaffirmation of love looked like and why was this extra step necessary?

We're about to focus on one of the most powerful words in all of *Christendom,* a word mentioned several times in verse 10. Jot it down in the margin.

In verse 11, what reason did Paul give for offering forgiveness?

Personal Response: Why do you think forgiveness protects us from being taken advantage of, or outwitted, by Satan? Give this some thought. If it helps you to think in opposite terms, how does not forgiving allow Satan a foothold in our relationships?

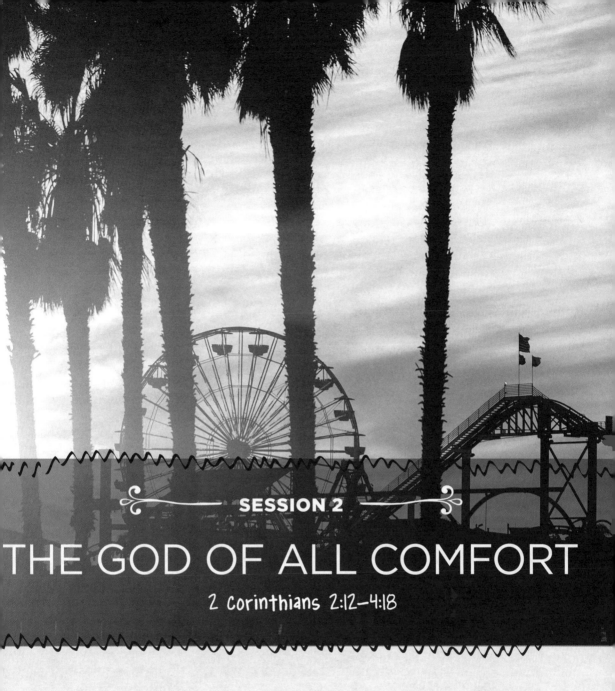

THE GOD OF ALL COMFORT

2 Corinthians 2:12–4:18

Cities can be the oddest places. They're this fusion of every type of creature under the sun converging in one spot for every conceivable activity under the sun. I was reminded of this after speaking at a women's retreat a couple of hours outside of Los Angeles. After the weekend, I headed back to the city for a few meetings, one of them in Santa Monica (please keep in mind that nearly 100 percent of my travels entail meetings not in places on the ocean). I had the day to walk the beach, the pier, and Third Street Promenade, and let me tell you Santa Monica has some characters— some real dramatic folk.

Some of them were in costumes, for unknown reasons, in the middle of the day. Two rollerbladers almost took me off this earth while blazing by me at cheetah speed. The people stretching on the beach intrigued me, especially the ones who got into particularly interesting positions showcasing their flexibility, or soul liberation, or things I don't think they should be showcasing. Of course there were also students, shoppers, tourists—the celebrities who I never laid eyes on despite my stealthy efforts—and people like me who were simply looking for a place to get frozen yogurt with fresh mango. On further thought, I may have been the only person looking for this.

The only problem was that no one looked all that happy. (This is often true in any city.) It has taken me many years to realize that fun and genuine happiness aren't all that closely related after all, and that all you could ever want is not really all you ever wanted. I strolled the city with a leisurely California gait, but inside I felt like I was trying to bat back the waves of heaviness rolling around me with a fly swatter. A sea of people seeking happiness and beachy sunshine—or maybe celebrity status—who didn't look like they'd found it.

As I continued walking and people-watching, I considered the good news of Jesus' salvation—what we often refer to as the gospel. This city of lonely faces clearly needed it, as do all cities. Why? Because cities are where the masses live.

Over the past few years I've been so stirred for the gospel's good news to get to the ends of the earth; the Amazon and Moldova are two areas I'm passionate about. Oh, but the ends of this earth include the house next door, the schools we attend, theatre districts, boardwalks, five-star hotels, the projects, and everything in between. To be honest with you, this presents a challenge for me. I often feel more at ease sharing the gospel with orphans or an Indian tribe in a far away land than I do with the actress, teacher or, for that matter, any of the beach stretchers. Maybe I respond this way because all these city people are, in a sense, my people. And ministering to your friends, neighbors, and family members has a way of getting awfully personal.

Sharing about my relationship with Jesus in the community I live in, is an entirely vulnerable experience. Some think the gospel package is too narrow, others find it offensive or irrelevant. A few really hate what's inside. Most, regardless of how they feel about what's in the box, at least want to know if your life resembles its contents. Maybe this is why Paul placed such an emphasis on the steadfast characteristic of sincerity.

I don't get to drop the news of Jesus off on someone's doorstep and then dash away from the questions and criticisms that people in the city are educated enough to fire at me. And I'm not even talking about the inquiries delivered out of spite. Rather it's questions born from the genuine wounds of kindhearted unbelievers: *Why didn't my parent get healed when I prayed? How come Christians are so judgmental? The church really hurt me as a kid. Why would God have allowed my abuse? Why is Jesus the only way? Can't we all just believe what we want and love one another?*

You can see how tempting it is—as the Sunday school song goes—to hide your light under a bushel. The truth is, when you talk about Jesus in the context of the place you live, people start watching you with those interrogating eyes. They want to get to the bottom of all this God-talk—to see if your faith rings true. When hardship befalls our friends, they want to know what our prayers can do for them. When trials befall us, they want to see how we'll walk through the valley. We often wonder: *Will I say the right thing? Have the right answer? What if I don't explain the gospel well?*

And then there are the many who are drawn to the life-changing grace of Jesus! Those just dying—some literally—for someone to show up in their lostness as a minister of reconciliation, an ambassador for Jesus. They'll rip into the box with vigor, paper sailing everywhere, like they've been waiting for the delivery of this good news all of their lives. But you know what this means? Hands-on discipleship time. So you still don't get to leave the package and run.

Do you see how personal all this is? How ministry in the city, in your community, in your church will crawl into every crevice of your life and faith?

This is precisely what I've loved about studying 2 Corinthians. Paul and his co-laborers served in Corinth, in the complications of a wealthy, artistic, athletic and commercial society. The sway of political power was real, the pull of wealth grueling. Social status was central to one's worth, and intellectualism relentlessly took Paul's spiritual wisdom to task. Every inch of the gospel gets tried and tested in a city like Corinth, as it does in our cities today. The good news, you ask? God has made you competent for the adventure in this place we call the city.

Group Guide (Week 2)

Prepare

As you review and prepare to meet and discuss the homework from 2 Corinthians 1:1—2:11, you'll address what you studied last week in the Session 1 homework about sincerity and suffering. Take a look at your notes and highlight anything that stood out that you might want to share with the group. Pray for God to work in your heart and to give you an even better understanding of 2 Corinthians after this time of group discussion.

Review & Discuss

You've already learned about the context of 2 Corinthians, but take a few minutes to consider what the church at Corinth was like. Why is it important for us to know where, when, and to whom Paul was writing (Day 1)? Then discuss the following questions.

Describe a situation when someone brought you much needed comfort because God ministered to them in a trial similar to your own.

We'll make a bit of a transition here as we move from talking about sincerity to a discussion of suffering. Take a look at the following benefits of suffering. Generally, we have a negative perspective on suffering, especially in the midst of it, but God is faithful to comfort us and to draw us closer to Himself during those times. We need to be mindful of these benefits and encourage others when they walk through difficulties.

Benefits of Suffering:
- We fellowship and identify with Jesus in a special way
- We receive comfort that flows through Jesus
- We comfort others
- We shift our dependence on ourselves to depending on God

In Day 2, we discussed the benefits of sufferings. Reflect on those as a group and encourage others in their sufferings. Journal any other benefits you can think of here.

Do you have an example of a situation in your life or a friend's life when you saw the benefits of suffering and a deeper dependence on God?

In Session 1's homework, we also studied sincerity in Day 3 and Day 4. Take a few minutes to take the following *How Sincere Am I?* quiz. Respond to each of the following questions with the word *never, rarely, occasionally,* or *often,* sharing other thoughts you have with the group as well.

- *Do I manipulate the truth to get something I want, avoid difficult situations, or try to make myself look better?*

- *Am I straightforward in my commitments and responses so that others know what I'm really thinking?*

- *Do the people around me trust my heart and integrity, even when I've hurt them?*

- *Do I often say one thing but mean another?*

- *Can I say my conscience is clear before God?*

This quiz will help us to examine our character to see how honest we are. It should also reveal areas in our lives where we need to be more Christlike.

Journal
Reflect on what you learned and studied last session in 2 Corinthians 1:1— 2:11. Consider how God might be preparing you for a deeper sincerity and commitment. This might be a personal commitment, or it could be God leading you to serve regularly at your church. Be sure to examine your heart and the motives behind your serving and take any commitments you make seriously.

Take Action
Seek out opportunities to comfort those who are suffering. List at least three ideas for helping those at your church or in your school or neighborhood who are experiencing difficulty.

- **Memorize:** 2 Corinthians 4:17
  Record yourself reading 2 Corinthians 4:17 aloud. Replay it throughout the week as you strive to commit this verse to memory.

DAY 1
The Fragrance of Christ *(2 Cor. 2:12-17)*

We're about to embark on a short section of our letter, but one that is full of emotion. Scholars have noted that 2 Corinthians is the most deeply personal and passionate of Paul's letters. The opportunity to peer into Paul's dialogue with the Corinthians allows us a unique window into the longings of his heart. Today, we'll see that Paul was exceedingly human, affected by the same relational concerns as us. We'll also find that decisions were not always clear to him—he had to seek God's direction and work hard like we do.

Read 2 Corinthians 2:12-17.

Where had God opened a door for Paul?

One of the reasons Paul was intent on finding Titus was because Titus had visited Corinth and would be able to tell him how the Corinthians received his letter. Were they angry? Had they cut him off? Had they repented or retaliated? Were they loyal to the false teachers, or had they turned back to God and therefore to Paul as their leader?

Paul said that he had no rest in his spirit, or "peace of mind" (v. 13). Can you identify with how nearly impossible it is to concentrate, help others, or do homework when your mind is on something else?

Paul made quite a leap from having found no rest and leaving for Macedonia in verse 13 to the beginning of verse 14. In the margin, write out the first five words of verse 14.

After verse 13, Paul took a five-chapter break from this storyline, picking back up in chapter 7. This will be important to keep in mind, otherwise the next few chapters will seem out of place. Go ahead and skip to 2 Corinthians 7:5-7.

Using these verses, list everything that likely caused Paul to thank God as he did in 2 Corinthians 2:14.

Perhaps when Paul wrote about leaving Troas for Macedonia it sparked his memory of reconnecting with Titus. This was where Titus told Paul about the Corinthians' change of heart toward him. While not everything was perfect, a major shift had taken place in Paul's relationship with the Corinthians, and he knew all thanks could be directed to none other than God Himself.

Finish writing out verse 14, which you started earlier in the margin.

We're not from Roman culture and have little context to draw from when it comes to a Roman parade, but Mardi Gras might be somewhat comparable. The Greek word *thriambeuō* means to be led in triumphal procession. In Paul's day, the Romans were known for their grand processions through the streets after significant battle victories.

Part of the Roman processional included incense bearers who marched carrying incense baskets and burners that spread the aroma of the victory.[1] I love this imagery because Paul reveals that we're constantly spreading the aroma of Christ! Last night, I ran into an acquaintance at the grocery store. She cannot stand the idea of Christianity, but she likes me well enough. As we caught up I was praying that I'd be a peaceful presence in her life, a scent that smelled like Jesus even if her heart was opposed. I ended up in the cheese aisle, which was a different scent altogether, but I think you get the point. Everywhere we go, at all times, we are spreading the aroma of Jesus.

According to verses 15-16, what do the people around us think of the fragrance of Christ?

I find it troubling that this aroma isn't so pleasing to some. The part of me that wants to be liked, to win friends and be admired, would prefer to wear one surefire fragrance that every person is drawn to. I'd like to know I've got the hit scent, all of the time. The sobering reality is that the fragrance of Christ is glorious to those who desire Him as Savior, but to those who have rejected Him, the scent is repulsive. Paul spoke to this in his earlier letter of 1 Corinthians.

Read 1 Corinthians 1:18,22-24. Why is the person of Jesus desirable to some and offensive to others?

Will I unashamedly wear the scent of Christ even when it's unpopular? In many schools or communities to wear the fragrance of Jesus means being labeled exclusive, a hater, reckless, uneducated, simple-minded, or narrow-minded. Oh, but thank God, if in the midst of these accusations we can exude the fragrance of Christ with humility and selflessness. You may be in a school or family life situation where the backlash you're enduring for being a Jesus-follower feels nearly overwhelming. You're in good company. Did you notice at the end of 2 Corinthians 2:16 that even Paul asked, who in the world is sufficient (or equal) to a task like this?

I believe the answer to his rhetorical question is that none of us are up for this. We all want to be liked, or we're prideful and want to be right. Either way, we need God's power to unashamedly stand for His Son. As we close today's study, we'll find that the final verse of chapter 2 gives us a hint.

According to verse 17, what did and didn't Paul do that separated him from so many others?

We must examine our motives. Sometimes we "preach God's Word" to win arguments, tear others down, or feel good about ourselves. No matter which of these, or other misguided motive, is true for us, they all lead to selfish gains.

Paul preached Jesus without using tricks or gimmicks—without pride, without selfishness, but rather in love, with compassion, with no hidden agenda—for their good.

Paul made it clear that the fragrance of Christ would be a foul smell of offense to some, because the cross of Christ is an insult to our pride. But what if we, the church, were to proclaim Jesus with sincerity? I dare say a great many more would be drawn to His love, curious to know what is so different about us.

Personal Response: I encourage you to close today's study by asking God to make you more sincere, especially as it relates to how you share Him with others.

DAY 2
Written on Our Hearts *(2 Cor. 3:1-6)*

Before we begin, remember the Scripture Paul had available to him did not include the full 66 books we study today. I bring this up because Paul quoted the Bible throughout 2 Corinthians, his Bible being only the Old Testament. It's fascinating to watch him dip his ladle into the Old Testament and pour its contents into new covenant bowls. I'll show you what I'm talking about.

Read 2 Corinthians 3:1-3.

Paul desperately expressed to the Corinthians how much he loved them, and yet the beginning of chapter 3 finds him having to establish this fact again. Picture the scene: False teachers had infiltrated the church in Paul's absence, having armed themselves with man-made credentials. They were sowing seeds of discord in an attempt to overthrow Paul's claim of apostleship, even though he'd personally planted the church.

Read Acts 18:7-8, which describes an event that took place in Corinth. What did many of the Corinthians do?

Paul had ministered to Titius Justus, Crispus, and many other Corinthians—real people, with names and jobs, he'd personally led to Christ. And now some of these people were under the sway of self-proclaimed spiritual leaders who were cunningly casting doubt in their minds about Paul. Essentially, what Paul said on behalf of himself and his ministry partners was: *After all we've done for you, are you seriously asking for us to dig up some letters to vouch for us? I've suffered, I've pleaded, I've served you for free, I've traveled long distances, I've cried over you—what more could confirm our roles as God's leaders in your life?*

Read verses 2-3. List every detail given about who the Corinthians were to Paul and his ministry partners.

Now, let's look back with Paul into his Bible (our Old Testament) and see what he meant by writing on stone tablets.

Read Exodus 31:18, 32:15-16.

This is the account where God gave Moses the Ten Commandments for the people of Israel. Moses mentioned that the law of their covenant with God had been engraved on stone tablets "by the finger of God" (Ex. 31:18).

Remember, the law and commandments were given to God's people to show them how to live. They were not given as burdens, but as life-giving boundaries. Though they were meant to serve as a blessing, the laws themselves ultimately couldn't change the heart. Have you ever done or said the right thing while your thoughts were anything but holy? Let's watch how the Lord takes the goodness of the law and moves it into a more personal, intimate space—one that actually changes us.

Read Ezekiel 36:26-27.

What did the Lord promise to remove? What did He promise to give?

Personal Response: Why was it important for this transformation to take place? In other words, why wasn't the law enough?

I love how my friend Julie answered this question: "Because we need to be recreated, not just corrected or redirected."

Back to our text, 2 Corinthians 3:2-3.

Essentially Paul was saying: *You all want more proof of the integrity of our ministry (letters of recommendation), but don't you see that you are that proof? You're not a ministry project to us that we can check off our list; you're embedded on our hearts! Christ has so drastically changed your life that the people around you have taken notice. Unlike the false teachers among you, our ministry to you isn't validated by lifeless ink or based on religiously following rules from a cold tablet, but the work of the Holy Spirit that has transformed your hearts.*

Some of you may be thinking the Corinthians didn't seem like all that great of an endorsement for Paul's ministry; They were not exactly superstar Christians. Keep in mind that the Corinthians were new believers who'd responded radically to the message of salvation in Christ. They had a ways to go in their sanctification, but they were still Paul's spiritual children and had experienced genuine transformation through Christ.

Personal Reflection: If the Corinthians were Paul's letter of recommendation, to whom is your life a letter of recommendation? In other words, what mentors and leaders in the faith have poured into your life? Write them a note thanking them for how their ministry has changed you.

Sometimes I don't feel ready to lead or mentor. I'm not sure how to best lead the Bible studies I teach—or the most effective way to express my faith to my unbelieving friends. I don't always know what godly advice looks like in complex situations. But, maybe it is not about our capabilities; it's more about our availability and what Christ does in and through us.

Read 2 Corinthians 3:4-6.

> **We discover in verse 6 that our competence is for a purpose. God makes us competent as_____ of the new covenant.**

As I consider the first six verses of chapter 3, the relational aspect of ministry rises to the top. Think about the words Paul chose to describe our sacred calling: *letters, hearts, Spirit, new covenant, life*. All these words deal with connection, life, and living. Each one of us is called to be ministers of the new covenant. And this will require us to build relationships that will etch themselves across our hearts, because we will love and be loved deeply enough to leave a mark.

We can fear this kind of closeness, though. And when we allow the Spirit of the living God to lead us in relationships, versus just following a list of good rules, we won't have as much control over the outcome. Let's face it, deep relationships require energy and time, but in the end, relational ministry is the only real ministry there is. And it promises more joy than we could ever hope for.

Tomorrow, we'll learn more about the old and new covenant, the letter and the Spirit. But for now, I want you to find encouragement knowing our competency as ministers of the gospel does not rest on our abilities, but is found in God. He will give you what you need to serve in the most relational ministry: the ministry of the Spirit.

DAY 3
A New Ministry *(2 Cor. 3:7-18)*

The things in which we find joy, or delight, evolve over time. A barefoot toddler on the ocean's shore will marvel at a seashell as he brushes off the sand. When he's a boy he'll beam atop his dirt bike while popping a wheelie, believing there couldn't be anything more spectacular. And one day, chances are, he'll stand nervously at the altar, his gaze locked on his bride at the end of the aisle. The glory will increase and so will his capacity for it. Something grander than a seashell and a dirt bike will have dawned, but who could have whispered that to the toddler on the sand or the boy on his bike in mid-air?

Glory is a difficult word to describe, but we know it inherently. A western sky at dusk is the glory of the sun. An October tree on fire with color is the glory of autumn. The face of Christ is the glory of God (2 Cor. 4:6). One thing we know for sure is that degrees and increments of glory exist. Today, we will look at the glory that increased from the old covenant to the new—and will increase until Christ's return.

With this in mind, read 2 Corinthians 3:7-11.

> **List the two words Paul used to describe these ministries (vv. 7-9).**
>
> **What accompanied both ministries, even though they are so different from one another? (The word is used several times in vv. 7-11.)**

To pull this together, the ministry of the old covenant was characterized by death, condemnation, and what would ultimately kill us. The ministry of the new covenant is characterized by the Holy Spirit, righteousness, and life. One of the glaring differences between the two ministries is that the old covenant could only show us our sin, whereas the ministry of the new covenant brings us a remedy for it.

> **Personal Reflection: Describe a time when you lived under a sense of condemnation, or an internal "death sentence," that you were powerless to change.**

As I write this study, I can't help but think of the shame I've felt at times, trying to be the good pastor's kid while feebly trying to avoid the wayward passions so many of us struggle with at times. I knew what a godly Christian life was supposed to look like (the law), but I was falling short of that standard and felt powerless to change (condemnation). You could say I was stuck under the glory of old covenant rules. You may ask, how in the world is the word *glory* attached to feeling hopelessly sinful?

We know from the Book of Galatians that the law (God's perfect standard) is meant to point us to Jesus (Gal. 3:19-26). I can testify that the painful realization of my inability to purify my own heart was glorious because this is what ultimately led me to my Savior, who is even more glorious. If this is still a bit unclear, let's keep pressing on.

I've noticed that we occasionally move so far into a culture of grace that we dismiss the Old Testament law as negative and something to be discarded. Remember that the law God gave to His people defined good and evil and instructed them how to live. The law God gave was good and accompanied by glory. However, ultimately it couldn't save us.

According to Romans 8:3 and Galatians 2:21, why couldn't the law give us life?

I want you to notice another important word that was used four times in 2 Corinthians 3:7-9. The word *ministry* will help us frame Paul's message in terms of how our lives should be characterized.

George Guthrie speaks of the word *ministry* this way: "The word could be used to speak of 'aid,' 'service', 'support,' 'an office,' an 'assignment,' or 'mediation.' Paul uses the term for work done in the service of Christ and for Christ's church."[2] I emphasize this word because Christ followers are all called to be ministers of His Gospel. And if we're to be about this ministry, we need to know what it looks like. Paul differentiated between Moses' ministry, which relayed a good law that was powerless to change the condition of our hearts, and the new ministry that brings righteousness and life!

So, what does this mean for us? First, it means we're not grumpy Jesus-servants calling out everyone who doesn't measure up to a righteous standard. Instead, we show the people around us the devastating reality that no one measures up and the glorious truth that Jesus meets the measures perfectly for us through His new ministry (Rom. 3:23-24)! It means we're no longer slaves to our sin—Jesus has made things new—and therefore we have a ministry that delivers freedom to those stuck in shame and failure. It means we're not doling out rules, rather we're offering the Holy Spirit who changes us and enables us to love and obey God. Do you see the difference between these two "ministries"?

According to today's passage, the glory of the old covenant, though good, was temporary and unable to fix the condition of sinful hearts. But the glory of the new covenant ministry is eternal. The new ministry doesn't just show us what we need to do to become right with God, it makes us righteous.

Read 2 Corinthians 3:12-18.
What is the only way the veil can be removed (vv. 14,16)?

According to verse 12, the new ministry gives us a hope and makes us _____?

When I consider verse 12, I realize the degree I hope in the good news of Jesus is the degree I let my testimony shine; the degree I've lost hope in the gospel is the degree I fail to let the light of Christ shine in my life. This reminds me of a conversation a Christian friend of mine and I had with another friend, Helen, who believes any sincere belief eventually leads to God. In Helen's estimation, if Jesus is the way for you, great, but if it's Buddha or Mohammed, that works too. I couldn't have been more proud of my friend's unveiled testimony, who in response to this false belief said, "Helen, you know how much I love you." Then with tears in her eyes she continued, "but that is a lie. There is no other way to God except through Jesus." Because only in Christ is the veil removed.

If Moses put a veil over his face to cover his fading glory, Paul said we're to live with unveiled faces to behold God's glory. This is what I want!

Read Hebrews 9:15.

Moses was the mediator of the old covenant, but Christ is the mediator of the new! When we look to Him, the veil over our hearts is removed, our sins are forgiven, and we are given a new heart inhabited by His Spirit. Since the veil over our hearts has been removed, let us also pull back the veil over our faces so we can confidently tell others the news that is so gloriously good.

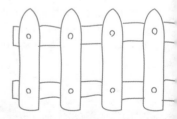

DAY 4
The Truth in Broad Daylight *(2 Cor. 4:1-6)*

One of the reasons I chose to study and teach 2 Corinthians was because of how I relate to it personally. The Holy Spirit used today's portion of Scripture to lead me to where I'm at now, a place of peace. I couldn't have found this place on my own. We just can't trust our passions, agendas, or wills unless they line up with God's revealed Word. God has taken that Word, over and over again, and redirected my steps to align with His path.

Read 2 Corinthians 4:1-2.

Paul renounces, or doesn't do, four things (v. 2). List these in the margin.

I want you to see these four words in the original Greek for a clearer picture:

Kryptos: Hidden or Secret. Concealed, private, inward
Aischynē: Shameful. Disgraceful
Panourgia: Deception. Crafty, cunning, false wisdom
Doloō: Distortion. To corrupt, ensnare, or handle deceitfully. This word "primarily signifies 'to ensnare;' hence, 'to corrupt,' especially by mingling the truths of the Word of God with false doctrines or notions, and so handling it 'deceitfully.'"[3]

One of the greatest signs of trouble is when we think we have to keep something a secret. Keeping confidences is one thing, but when we feel the need to keep a behavior or relationship under cover, not only do we have a major problem, but we've also traded in our freedom. That's the really sneaky thing about sin—it advertises liberty with all its promised fun, but the moment you bite you're a slave to its rules. Eventually it requires maintaining a tight cover, everything under wraps, so nobody will know. Too many people I know are facing secret things bubbling to the surface that are fracturing otherwise beautiful relationships. Everything can be traced back to an ensnaring sin, which led to shame, which in turn required secretive behavior. This is the Enemy's specialty.

Read 1 Corinthians 4:5 where Paul wrote about what would happen to the secret things we harbor. What will the Lord do when He comes?

What do Luke 12:2 and Romans 2:29 have in common with the verse you just read?

When a person we know or love is keeping something from us, but tells us there's nothing going on, it can make us feel positively crazy. Confusion brews because what we're getting from the other person is something the Bible calls bad fruit, but we may not be able to find the tree. In other words, we see the behavior, but we can't see the root or what causes it. Rather than go on a spree of judgment, we can take great comfort in knowing that God sees the heart. Nothing is hidden from Him.

Secrecy, shameful ways, deception, and distortion all overlap, but they hold their own places of meaning. Something that really jumped out at me was what distortion is attached to in this particular passage.

Paul said he did not distort _____.

Paul was reacting to the false teachers in Corinth. They were harming the church by distorting God's Word and deceptively covering up shameful behavior, perhaps in the name of Christendom. Paul was saying: *Look, this is not the way my fellow ministers and I have ever treated you.*

Distortion of God's Word plays out in many ways. However, I most often see these two forms: bending the Word to either condemn a behavior it doesn't or to condone a behavior it doesn't. In Paul's day, the false teachers twisted the sacred Scriptures to condone whatever greed, immorality, and power struggles they wanted to engage in. The very same thing is happening today, and we desperately need discernment from the Holy Spirit and knowledge of the Word to have eyes to see what's happening around us.

Personal Reflection: Have you ever uselessly tried to get a person (or group of people) to approve of you? Explain.

If we can absorb this into the core our beings, our lives will take a turn for peace. Too often, I've strained to live my life for the approval of others, rather than live openly before God. But this is changing. I still care what people think, but I'm more concerned with what God thinks. I'm finding peace in living this way, even if it means being misunderstood in the eyes of men.

Read 2 Corinthians 4:3-6.

Even though Paul lived with a clear conscience in front of others and in the sight of God, not everyone acknowledged this. What explanation did Paul give for why people don't always the see gospel light in our lives (vv. 3-4)?

According to verse 4:5, what does Paul preach to the Corinthians and why do you think he emphasizes this?

I have this verse written on a note card that is leaning against my desk lamp. This is a reminder I need, because it can be easy to preach myself and so hard to be a servant. We live in a celebrity culture where an obsession with self, pride, notoriety, and fame is everywhere. Even in Christian ministry. While I am not immune to this struggle, I experience great freedom when my heart's desire is to share Jesus without being worried and concern with myself. It's like dropping 50 pounds worth of self-awareness off your back. It's grand.

As Paul presented his case before the Corinthians, he continually pointed back to Jesus. It would have been easy for him to rest on his good conscience or upright ministry. But he didn't bank on his wit, charm, or goodness to give credit to his ministry. Only Christ.

Compare verses 3:7 and 4:6, and circle the common word that is connected to both Christ and Moses.

Power   Radiance   Face   Countenance

I want you to know that no matter where you have been, what you have covered up, or what you are struggling with, you have access to the glory of God. Just this morning I was reminded that we're able to draw near to God, not because He turns a blind eye to our sin, but because His Son's blood was shed for us on the cross and our consciences have been washed clean (Heb. 10:19-25). Will you repent of whatever deceit, distortion, or shameful or hidden ways you're harboring, to get a fresh look at the face of Christ? This is where all the glory is.

DAY 5
Fixing Our Eyes on Jesus *(2 Cor. 4:7-18)*

We're nearing the end of Session 2. If you've wondered what your pain is worth or if any real purpose could accompany your sufferings, or if you're hurting so deeply you're not sure you care either way, well then—these verses are for you.

Read 2 Corinthians 4:7-18.

On my desk sits a burgundy, leather King James Bible, a weighty gavel of a book as opposed to the lighter and smaller editions that can slip in your purse. This Bible was given to me by my youth group leaders on my sixteenth birthday. I just slid it out from underneath a pile of books and commentaries and quietly opened it, because sometimes the best way to reach back into personal seasons of pain is to find the Bible you carried while you lived them.

The imagery in verse 7 is particularly meaningful to me. I often feel inadequate and weak in ministry and relationships, wishing I could be a stronger, more put-together vessel through whom the Lord displays His power. But Paul said we hold the treasure of knowing Christ in a clay jar, which was a widely used vessel of the time. Clay jars were ordinary, fragile, commonplace. This metaphor points to our weakness and fragility but not our insignificance, as we'll see more clearly in chapter 13.

> **Personal Response: Look again at verse 7. Why is it important that the treasure of Christ's light is housed in weak vessels?**

The Corinthians had accused Paul of not being a true apostle because of his suffering and weakness. Their thought process probably went something like this: *If Paul is really God's man why is he such a poor speaker? Why does he suffer so much?* You may be going through a hardship or struggling with certain weaknesses. And it may be easy to think that if God really had His hand on you, then you wouldn't be hurting so much and you'd certainly be stronger than you are. But it's through our weaknesses that the power of Christ shines most brightly. Dear struggler, don't berate yourself for being an earthen vessel, rather rejoice that the light of Christ is most brilliant in your weakness. The Lord knows how fragile we are (Ps. 103:13-14).

In verses 8-9 Paul generally described some of his extraordinary trials, yet an important conjunction followed each one—the word *but*. The suffering Paul experienced was limited in what it could ultimately do to him.

Draw a line between the corresponding statements.

Hard pressed, troubled, afflicted   But not destroyed

Perplexed   But not abandoned

Persecuted   But not in despair

Struck down   But not crushed

Which one of these pairings means the most to you and why? For instance, right now I'm perplexed about something I'm struggling with; it's pretty painful at times. But I can honestly say I am not in despair over this situation because the Lord has given me encouragement and peace.

When it comes to the pain we experience, we may not always consider how it will ultimately minister to others. And how often do we consider whether or not the life of Jesus is being revealed through our suffering? Most of the time we're just trying to make it through. But Paul desperately wanted life to be brought to the Corinthians as a result of His suffering. He wanted Jesus to be revealed to them through the weakness of his body. And in verse 15, he said his suffering was all for their benefit! This is others-centered to the core, and you get the distinct impression it was his joy.

Let's sum up Paul's view of suffering from verses 10-12: The highest desire in the midst of our suffering is for Jesus to be revealed in us, for the sake of others, for the glory of God. Don't despair if you're not there yet. I'm not either. But my heart's desire is more along these lines than it used to be. If I'm going to walk through the valley, I want to know it will count for God's kingdom and His people.

Girls, I can't think of a better way to end our week than with verses 16-18. Look at what Paul said at the beginning of verse 16 and fill in the blanks. As a result of everything we've studied today,

"Therefore ____ ____ _____ _____ _____."

Even though we are outwardly aging, what is happening inside believers' souls on a daily basis?

I love how one scholar says that our trials are producing for us an eternal measure of glory that is breathtaking![4] Our sufferings are anything but in vain. As we walk (or limp, or are carried) through our sufferings, they mysteriously achieve a glory for eternity—a glory so awe-inspiring that our most weighty struggles seem incredibly short-lived. This is not to passively dismiss the very real pain and devastation so many experience—Paul himself took great pains to list his profound sufferings and did so throughout his ministry. His encouragement was that no matter how deep the pain drives us here on earth, it will one day explode into breathtaking glory without end.

Yes, it is all about Jesus shining through our weakness, for the benefit of others, to the glory of God. But in verse 17, Paul let us know our suffering is not without reason. I'm thankful the Lord doesn't forget or dismiss our very real pain. He's preparing an eternal glory for us.

You're a third of the way through 2 Corinthians! I'm so proud of you. This letter is not particularly light, but if we apply what we've learned we'll find it immensely practical. I've had to remember that Christ shines brightly through me, even in seasons when I'm perplexed or hard pressed. This letter challenges me to share my faith more boldly and more often, to let more people know what I believe and why I believe it—to pull back the veil from my countenance since Jesus has taken it off my heart. I've been encouraged to see my struggles and trials in light of eternity, knowing as I surrender them to the Lord, He's investing their momentary existence into an eternal load of future glory.

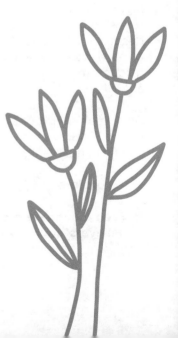

SESSION 3

A NEW MINISTRY

2 Corinthians 5:1–7:1

My friends Mike and Patricia used to live in the southern part of Brazil where they started a remarkable ministry for kids called Open Arms. One delightful February afternoon on the Amazon's Rio Negro (delightful means molten humidity), Mike and I were having an intriguing chat. We were discussing the challenge, particularly prevalent in developing societies, of motivating people toward a goal they see no reason to attain. He told me about a little known village he discovered that sat in the middle of a mango plantation. The trees dripped with more mangos than the people could possibly consume. The branches bowed with bright and bulging fruit, dangling by slender stems, like oversized Christmas lights strung through the village. It could make a California fruit stand jealous.

Most of the people in the village had a form of shelter over their heads and just enough food to scrape together for the day's needs. A speared fish for dinner and a peeled mango fresh off the tree could round out a plate. But their plight, though serious, could have been improved. Poverty ruled the day, even in the midst of clusters of mangos that could be sold for significant profit. But most went uneaten, hurling to the ground, rotting in the heat, and eventually seeping back into the soil.

Mike suggested that the village create a dehydration operation that could produce dried mangos, then export them to other parts of the country. If the people could just capitalize on the natural resources they were sitting on, or more literally sitting under, they could produce revenue; this would lead to opportunities for their children, storehouses for lean times, and generally a far better life. They could potentially escape from poverty.

Mike presented his idea to several of the leaders in the community and the response was generally the same, "Why would we want to do that?" Their lack of desire had nothing to do with lack of smarts or abilities, rather it was scarcity of exposure and vision. They had no picture in their minds of what life could look like other than the one they knew—a life peppered with disease and alcoholism, plagued by boredom that stems from poverty, and characterized by a lack of education. This was acceptable to them because they didn't know what else was out there. Industriousness and a business plan seemed like silly ideas, because why go to all that trouble when you've already got a mango in your hand?

As Mike told the story, my inner American opportunist was jumping up and down, anxious for this village to see what they were missing. Putting the numerous mangos to work for a better life was far superior to one mango tiding you over until the next meal. That was when I saw myself square in the eyes of the people Mike portrayed. I'm far too easily satisfied with the familiar pleasures right in front of me, even though I know they are temporary. I find my delight in worldly stuff, even though Jesus told us we're to store up treasures that will last, not spend our precious moments on earth focused on what is fading. The path of least resistance, though, is to just get by. In other words, we're satisfied to live mango to mango. Like the village in Brazil, we are made for exceedingly more, but it requires faith to live for the more that lies ahead.

In this session, we'll find Paul talking about a world we haven't been to yet, one he called by the most grounding word my heart knows: home. "To be away from the body is to be at home with the Lord," he said. And as our eyes are opened to this unseen world and the Savior who reigns in it, we'll want to live our lives here in view of what will be. We won't be satisfied with the lean pleasures that make promises today but wither tomorrow. We'll know and trust the Word when it says that a life far superior is not only to come, but can be grasped right now as we walk with Christ.

As C.S. Lewis put it, "It would seem that Our Lord finds our desires not too strong, but too weak. We are half-hearted creatures, fooling about with drink and sex and ambition when infinite joy is offered us, like an ignorant child who wants to go on making mud pies in a slum because he cannot imagine what is meant by the offer of a holiday at the sea. We are far too easily pleased."[1] I don't want to be too easily pleased. And, since you're digging into 2 Corinthians, I don't think you want to be either. Throughout this session, we have the opportunity to have our eyes opened to a glimpse of what's to come. We'll be reminded that each of us will give an account for how we've lived our lives on earth, but this doesn't have to be a fearful thing. As we invest our lives for Jesus Christ on this earth—enduring hardship with joy, boldly sharing our faith, generously giving our money and time to those in need, serving in our local church—we'll be doing so in light of an unchangeable promise: He has gone to prepare a place for us greater than anything we've seen or can imagine. May we not be too easily satisfied with the stuff we can see, simply because it's all we know. More than mangos are ripe for the harvest.

Group Guide (Week 3)

Prepare

Ask God to use your weaknesses for His glory and to give you confidence in Him, not in things of this earth. Pray for discipline to read and study His Word and that you will continually fix your eyes on Him.

Review & Discuss

Review what you studied and learned in Session 2's homework. Circle or journal about anything you might want to bring to this time of group discussion. If you have the time, read the intro on the previous three pages for Session 3. Discuss the following questions with your group.

What does the fragrance of Christ look like on a person? Explain.

How hopeful are you in Jesus, and therefore how bold?

Paul zigzagged like a nomad all over the place, facing great hardships and uncertainties. Yet, he could thankfully and confidently state he was led in God's triumphal procession in Christ. How does this truth encourage you during seasons when you can't figure out where your life is going, or when hardship seems to endure forever?

Fill in the blanks to learn more about the old and new covenants (v. 6): The letter (law) _____, but the Spirit gives _____.

If we're to appreciate the ministry of the new covenant, we have to understand how hopeless our situation would be without Christ. We have to feel the weight of coming up short of a perfect standard (old covenant) that by its very nature could not stoop to meet our sinful shortcomings. When we truly grasp this, we'll be overwhelmed that God's Son humbled Himself to save us, accomplishing for us what the law never could (Phil. 2:8).

Read Philippians 2:8 aloud and discuss what Jesus accomplished for us that only He could do.

How does Paul's declaration that he ministered to the Corinthians in the sight of God free you to live and serve transparently before Him, rather than seeking the approval of others?

Are there any relationships or areas in your life where you are the focus and your agenda is first? Share what changes you need to make with someone who will hold you accountable.

All of us have either been through or witnessed profound suffering that seemed to go on forever. How is it that Paul could call his suffering light and momentary?

What are some practical steps we can take to fix our eyes on what is unseen?

Journal

Journal a prayer of thanksgiving for a relationship in your life that God has restored. Or, write a prayer asking God to redeem a broken relationship you long to see restored.

Take Action

Kelly said we are to rejoice that the light of Christ is most brilliant in our weaknesses. In what ways do you need to rejoice in your weaknesses this week?

Consider whether you are distancing yourself from serving God in a way that requires commitment. If so, why? Spend time confessing this to the Lord and asking for courage to change directions.

- **Memorize:** 2 Corinthians 5:21
  Consider listening to "Jesus Messiah" by Chris Tomlin (*Passion: Awakening [Deluxe Edition]*, Sparrow, 2010) throughout the week as a tool to help you memorize this verse. Make a mental note of where this Scripture comes in as you listen to the lyrics.

DAY 1
Home *(2 Cor. 5:1-9)*

As I grow older, I'm more aware of little things like how difficult it is to bend down a bunch of times while picking up the house, or the shady half-moons under my eyes when I wake up in the morning, and a forehead that folds into creases when I do things like smile. I'm trying to slow this whole train down, but it seems to be oddly picking up speed. And even when I find a great concealer, the reality is that it may help me look better for my age, but it won't make me look like I'm seventeen.

So there's my confession. I don't love this idea of "outwardly ... wasting away," that we closed with last week. I'm all for the inward renewal of the spirit, I just wish I could get both body and spirit tracking in the same positive direction. In a sense, this will one day happen, but instead of the body evolving over time into a superior vessel, it will be redeemed in a moment, totally glorified without an exercise program to achieve it. Girls, since most of you are too young to relate—with all your natural beauty and supple skin—just enjoy your youth and tuck this away. It will come in handy one day.

As you read 2 Corinthians 5:1-5, keep in mind the following definitions:
- Earthly tent = physical body
- Eternal house/building (not built with human hands) = resurrection body
- Nakedness = soul without a body
- Clothed = soul with a body

Paul's main purpose here wasn't to describe heaven in detail, but to show his accusers that the suffering he went through didn't disqualify him from being an apostle—Paul's (and our) ultimate deliverance is yet to come. Yes, we have frail jars-of-clay bodies in this life, but we will one day receive an eternal, glorified body.

Personal Response: Why would Paul use the imagery of an earthly tent to describe our physical bodies (your version may say "dwelling," but go with tent)?

Read Hebrews 11:8-10.

Tents aren't that complicated to set up or tear down, and they're temporary in nature. Abraham and his family longed for the permanent dwelling place they knew the Lord had promised to them. In the meantime, they kept things as simple, flexible, and unattached as possible. In the same way, we're to take great care of

the earthly bodies God has given us, but we can never lose sight of the permanent home we're heading toward with Christ.

In verse 2, Paul used the word "groan" to describe our longing to be clothed with our heavenly dwelling. The Greek word for groan used here is *stenazō*, which indicates Paul's frustration with still being in this body, yet he says we groan in a hopeful kind of way. Paul's groaning wasn't out of despair, but based on an unshakable confidence and a yearning for a new body that won't be betrayed by age or accidents. Far more important, he groaned for perfect unity with Christ.

Here's what I'm wondering: Are we doing the wrong things with our groaning? What I mean is, as our bodies tire or become sick, does our groaning lead us to a bunch of earthly remedies (doctor's visits, medications, essential oils, etc.) as the ultimate answer? Or does it push us into a deeper pursuit of Jesus and a hope for what's to come? I want it to be the latter!

According to verse 3, when we're clothed we will no longer be _____.

I can't help but think of Adam and Eve in Genesis 3:7, after having just sinned by eating from the fruit of the tree of the knowledge of good and evil.

Do you remember what they instantly became aware of? Write it below. (If you're not sure, look up the reference.)

Read 1 Corinthians 15:53-54.

Turn back to today's text and look at the second half of 2 Corinthians 5:4. Keeping the verses you just read in mind along with this one, what does it appear will happen to the bodies we have now?

When the Lord clothes us with our heavenly bodies, notice He won't destroy the ones we have for new ones. This is significant: Paul's desire wasn't to be rid of an earthly body, but to have that body swallowed up by an eternal and immortal one. This truth encourages me to value and take care of my earthly body, while not putting my final hope in it because I know one day it will literally be engulfed by a new one.

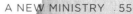

According to verse 5, how can we be certain that we will not be left naked and that our earthly bodies will eventually be completely robed in a new body?

We long to know, that in a world of questions and disappointment, there are anchors of certainty—especially when it comes to what will happen after we physically die. This is why we can't overstate how incredible it is that God has given us His very Spirit as a deposit to guarantee what is to come (2 Cor. 1:22; 5:5). The Lord did not have to guarantee us anything. But He knew we'd suffer in this life, as Paul suffered. He knew we'd question His promises. He knew our faith would wane when an agnostic teacher used observed evidence to seemingly throw out the foundations of our faith. The Lord knew we would need something to hold on to if we were going to make it. So He gave us a deposit: His Spirit.

Finish reading today's text, 2 Corinthians 5:6-9.

What was Paul's goal no matter where he called home (v. 9)?

I've often written about my love for the home. Friends gathered by the fireplace in winter or around the grill in July are some of my very favorite moments of life. In reality, home is not so much about a structure but the people that inhabit and color it. Did you notice that when Paul described what it means to be truly home, he didn't point to a place but a person? He pointed to the fact that "home" is with the Lord.

Paul went so far as to say that if given a choice he'd leave his body right then to experience the fullness of face-to-face relationship with Christ. I think one of the reasons we just don't think too deeply about eternal life is because we're not close enough with the Lord now for thoughts of being with Him in heaven to really be a comfort to us. We prefer to find our comfort in what's familiar here on earth, but Paul said home is all about where Jesus is.

Close today by reading John 14:1-4.

As you close today's study, consider that Jesus' statement was all about relationship: *I will come back and take you to be with me.* He would no longer be with them in the flesh, but He would give them His Spirit as a deposit: *Don't let your hearts be troubled.* The Spirit would be a comfort that would give us confidence: *Trust in God.* Taking us to be with Him. *Us with Him.* This, girls, is the home we've always longed for. And when we get there we'll be swept across the threshold in these same bodies, made totally new.

DAY 2
A Compelling Love *(2 Cor. 5:10-15)*

I grew up in a church setting where holiness and Christian behavior were emphasized. Grace was a vital part of the conversation when it came to needing it to get to heaven, but it wasn't talked about much when life got messy or just plain sinful. Usually, mistakes and messes just meant consequences. I'm sure my church experience was not isolated. In an effort to right the wrongs of the grace-for-heaven-only mentality, I've seen the church swing maybe too far in the other direction, where it's all grace at the expense of holiness or obedience. We've become so used to depravity that we're not all that bothered by it anymore. Sin just isn't what it used to be.

A proper tension exists here, doesn't it? We need grace all day long, and certainly there is forgiveness of sins and remarkable redemption of the past. However, to live any way we want under the premise of grace is to miss its gift. We don't talk about it all that much, but we will all stand before the judgment seat of Christ and give an account for how we lived our lives. Rest assured that if you're a believer in Jesus, this judgment seat has nothing to do with your salvation—that is Jesus' gift and is by grace and grace alone. Still, we need to know that we will be held accountable for our actions. What we do in this life matters.

Read 2 Corinthians 5:10-15.

What will all believers be judged on, according to verse 10?

Verse 10 is connected to yesterday's reading concerning what we choose to do while being at home in our earthy bodies. Are we doing what is good, or what is bad or worthless? Yes, we will have to give an account for the wrong we've done, but the Lord will also remember our sacrifices, obedience, love, and worship of Him. For the one who has veered off the path, this is an exhortation to repent and get back on track (1 John 1:9). For the weary and persecuted, this is great news! The Lord sees and will not forget all the good you are doing in His name (Gal. 6:9).

Personal Reflection: How does it challenge the way you make decisions to know you will stand before the judgment seat of Christ? How does it encourage you in your walk with Christ?

Paul stated that the fear of the Lord caused them to do something in particular (v. 11). What was it?

This is refreshing to me. Do you see what Paul was doing in this letter? He wanted the Corinthian church to understand that His ministry to them was born out of love and unselfish motives. Because he had a healthy, reverent fear of the Lord—knowing he would one day stand before Jesus to give an account—he lived openly before them. He had nothing to hide. He was not in ministry to get famous or rich.

Each of us is called to ministry in our schools, churches, and neighborhoods. As I write these words, I'm motivated to take inventory of the reason I serve others.

> **Personal Reflection: Ask the Lord to search your heart and reveal any areas where your service or discipleship is selfishly motivated. Jot down in the margin and confess anything He brings to mind. Then, ask God to create a pure heart in you.**

Some of the Corinthians based their respect on outward appearances (v. 12). Much like in our own day, the worldly Corinthians prized the power and prestige they could lay their eyes on. Paul's suffering, lack of wealth, lack of public speaking skills, and position in society caused many of the Corinthians to discount him. But Paul contended that there was something else to consider.

Some of the Corinthians questioned Paul's sincerity. To answer them, Paul further explained his others-centered ministry in verse 13. He described two states of mind or behaviors. To whom were each directed?

> **When Paul seemed out of his mind (or like a religious fanatic), it was for _____.**

> **When he was clear and soundly instructional, it was for _____.**

We're not exactly sure what Paul meant when he used the phrase "out of our mind." He may have been referring to the way people perceived his supernatural experiences, speaking in tongues, or an exceptional emotion toward God. Regardless, what's important is Paul's expression that whether in exceptional or sound behavior, it was all for God and the people he served. Nothing was for selfish gain.

It would be easy for us to perceive Paul's statements as arrogant, if not for verses 14-15. I mean, how many people can say they're constantly serving God and others? How many can confidently encourage others to look on the secret motivations of their hearts? The answer is, no one—apart from Jesus. So, let's close with these powerful verses.

Paul said the love of Christ _____ us (v. 14).

Different versions of the Bible offer different translations of the Greek word *synechō* (compels), all roughly meaning to hold together, hold completely, constrain, or compress. It can also mean to physically be held.[2] Simply put, when the love of Jesus is what's holding and compelling you, you will selflessly bless and serve others. Only then can our motivations be truly unselfish.
The next few sentences explain the theology behind this altogether tangible love of Christ.

What did Christ do to show this love, and who did He do it for?

Record verse 15 in the margin. Then, explain how we're called to live now based on Jesus' sacrifice for us.

All of 2 Corinthians is a treasure chest filled with the attributes of God, rich theology, wisdom for relationships, comfort, and encouragement, along with a host of other jewels. But it's possible that no single phrase in this letter has the power to entirely redirect our lives than this one: We're to no longer live for ourselves but for our Savior. We don't want this concept to be what pastor and author Eugene Peterson calls "godtalk"—lifeless, Christian terminology that sounds good but never takes root in our hearts.[3] What we need is for this to change us. Our hearts. Actions. Behaviors. Motivations.

Close with this challenge: *May the love of Jesus hold you with both hands, and as a result may you no longer live for yourself but for the One who gave His life for you*. Spend some time in prayer reaffirming your love for Jesus.

DAY 3
All Things New *(2 Cor. 5:16-21)*

Last Christmas I surprised my eight year-old niece, Maryn, with a bearded dragon. He's affectionately known as Oscar Michael Gates, because if our family is going to house a lizard it at least needs to be a distinguished one. (We may have just discovered that Oscar Michael is in fact a girl. Maryn has decided not to change her name; I don't know what to do about this). Besides Murphy the beagle, this was Maryn's first pet to have and to hold (and to feed live worms, crickets, and kale) until college do they part. My sister nearly died when I brought it home, but I figured she'd eventually grow accustomed to sheltering a reptile in her home. Seeing that I was flying back to Nashville a few days later, and bore zero responsibility other than being one fabulous aunt, I was ecstatic about my gift selection.

Since Christmas, my phone has been blowing up with pictures of Maryn feeding Oscar live creatures, bathing him in the sink, stroking and toting him all over the house. One night he watched a movie with the family—in my sister and her husband's bed. This makes me so happy. Maryn adores him like I knew she would. I'm starting to wonder if the Christmas Day that Oscar came will be a marker for her—life before and after his arrival.

I can think of a few dividing lines in my life, experiences that marked a before and after. Some were amazing, others painful. We may not consider this on a regular basis, but all of us living today are on the backside of history's most epic event: Christ's death and resurrection. In today's reading—what one scholar described as being "one of the most difficult and important passages of Paul's writing"[4]—we'll see how this historic dividing line can do nothing but change our thinking. I wish we were sitting across from one another, because no matter where either of us finds ourselves, I'd like to say to you, and you to me, "Friend, the old has gone, the new has come!"

Read 2 Corinthians 5:16-21.

The phrase "from now on" (v. 16) indicates a point in time where things will no longer be the same as they were.

> **How did Paul say that, from now on, we will look at people and Jesus differently than before? Now, look at verse 17. Why will we view Christ and others in a new way?**

Remember the Corinthian culture in which Paul ministered. The people bowed to power, social status, wealth, and prestige. People judged one another according to Hollywood standards. Like we discussed yesterday, the community judged by outward appearances rather than looking at people's hearts.

In verse 17, Paul draws our attention to a dividing line that's already taken place in history. Because of Jesus coming to earth, along with His death and resurrection, the old order of sin's regime that bound us under the law is in the past. All new things have come. We are new creations in Christ. This challenges me at two points of belief in particular: First, how much do I believe my life can change? Second, how much do I believe someone else's life can change?

Personal Reflection: Have you given up believing that you or someone else could change in a certain area? If so, write about your discouragement and why you lack hope in this area.

This is hits home for me. I know so many people right now who've decided that either they can't change or a person close to them can't change. Now I'm not talking about changing from an avid introvert to a people person, a brunette to a redhead. I don't have in mind a plump chef who's suddenly clearing hurdles as a track star. But what about the person with the anger or eating problem? Can a self-seeking student find her anchor and self-worth in God? Might the materially obsessed lay down his money down for the poor? Yeah, I think all this is absolutely possible, and a whole lot more. Remember—from now on—things are different! We no longer view others or ourselves through the frame of our sin and weakness, nor do we puff ourselves up solely on the basis of outward achievement. Things are new. Everything has changed since Jesus came into the world. We now have the very power that raised Christ from the dead working within us (Eph. 1:19-20).

What two words make this change possible? "Therefore if anyone is _____ _____." (v. 17)

Skim back over verses 18-21. Did you pick up on a key word? Jot it down in the margin.

We can't be put side-by-side against the goodness and purity of God without our sin being exposed, much like checking the answers to your math homework against the answers in the back of the book. When your answers are different from the correct answers in the back, you have to look at the math problem you worked to see what step you missed. The answers in the back of the book won't

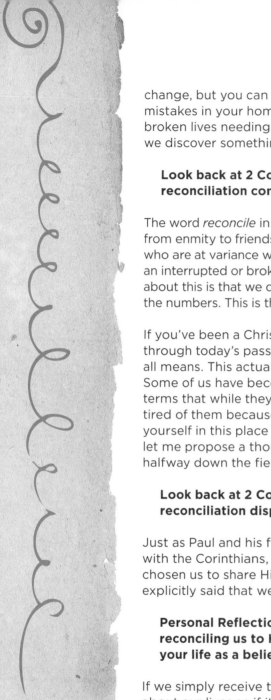

change, but you can use them to help you see how to correct the mistakes in your homework. But when it comes to our sinful and broken lives needing to be reconciled to God's perfect standard, we discover something altogether astounding here.

> **Look back at 2 Corinthians 5:18. From whom does reconciliation come? And who gets reconciled to whom?**

The word *reconcile* in Scripture means to change, exchange, change from enmity to friendship, to return to favor with, or to reconcile those who are at variance with God.[5] It can also mean "reestablishment of an interrupted or broken relationship."[6] What's so completely amazing about this is that we don't have to figure out a way to fill the gap or fix the numbers. This is the Lord's work.

If you've been a Christian for a long time, you may have whipped through today's passage on reconciliation, well-versed on what it all means. This actually may be a hindrance to us and the kingdom. Some of us have become so accustomed to certain theological terms that while they may be truths we're happy for, we've grown tired of them because we've heard them so many times. If you find yourself in this place of staleness over the gift of reconciliation, let me propose a thought: You may have only taken this passage halfway down the field.

> **Look back at 2 Corinthians 5:19-20. How was the message of reconciliation dispersed to the Corinthians?**

Just as Paul and his friends shared the message of reconciliation with the Corinthians, it's now our pleasure and task. God has chosen us to share His message with the people around us. Paul explicitly said that we are Christ's _____.

> **Personal Reflection: How does sharing the gospel (God reconciling us to Himself through the sacrifice of Jesus) keep your life as a believer fresh and exciting?**

If we simply receive the gift of reconciliation with God and go about our lives as if it's up to everyone else to figure it out for themselves, then we've missed the joy, the adventure, and the point altogether.

> **Personal Response: What keeps you from sharing the message of reconciliation with others? Confess these things and ask God to help you share His love and the need for reconciliation to the people around you.**

DAY 4
Living in the Tension *(2 Cor. 6:1-10)*

Read 2 Corinthians 5:21-6:2.

Let's begin with the last verse of yesterday's reading to remind us of the great grace God extended to us. In 2 Corinthians 6:1, Paul warned the Corinthians not to receive this grace in vain. The Greek word for vain is *kenos* and it means void, like an empty jug or building, or empty handed; useless or without effect.

Last week, I received a beautiful bouquet of flowers to cut and separate into jars. Except I never got around to the cutting and arranging part, and the whole bunch is rotting in murky water in my kitchen, the rubber band still around the stems. Crazy, right? This is what it means to receive something in vain. The quality of the gift hasn't changed. But my having it without fully receiving it was as good as setting empty jars all over the house. I had the flowers right there, but was not making full use of them.

In 2 Corinthians 6:2, we actually get two verses in one, because Paul drew from an Old Testament prophecy in Isaiah 49:8. Since this is so important to our understanding of concepts like grace, reconciliation, and salvation, I want you to read Isaiah 49:8-13. Keep in mind this was God's promise to His servant Jesus, but it also relates to the broader deliverance of God's people.

Turn back to 2 Corinthians and let's consider what Paul was saying. Pulling from Isaiah's words about how Jesus would bring salvation, Paul was also talking about when salvation would come.

> **Look at the second half of verse 2. When is the time of God's favor (acceptable time) and when is the day of His salvation?**

Do you sense the urgency in Paul's pen as he wrote out Isaiah's prophecy, understanding that the prophecy had been fulfilled in Jesus' life, death, and resurrection? It was for the Corinthians then, and it is for us now! The day of God's favor and the day of salvation are *right now* if you're still breathing. Cut the flowers. Get them in the jars. Don't receive His grace in vain.

Continue reading 2 Corinthians 6:3-10.

As we study this letter, we must remember the criticism Paul received. Misunderstandings and offenses abounded, even though Paul did everything he could to minimize them.

According to verse 3, what was he ultimately trying to protect?

Paul listed a number of trials he'd experienced along with some virtues he displayed in those sufferings, thanks be to the Holy Spirit. The challenging thing about lists is truly reading them, as opposed to just scanning them or checking certain items off them. I want us to resist the quick glance, to consider each description as an experience Paul actually walked through, maybe experiences you too will face.

Circle the general descriptions of Paul's trials below and square the specific ones (2 Cor. 6:4b-5):

Troubles   Hardships   Distresses   Beatings   Imprisonments

Riots   Hard work   Sleepless nights   Hunger

Keeping in mind all that Paul suffered, jot down the four virtues that characterized his life in the margin. Include the preposition in front of each description (2 Cor. 6:6a-7b).

We can be temped to look at these four virtues Paul displayed during his trials, lump them together in a hurry, and then conclude that Paul was one great guy. But let's look at these more closely to see the heart of this list.

- In this case, purity was the opposite of corruption. It can also mean simplicity of heart or sincerity. Paul's motives were pure before God and the Corinthians. He wanted what was best for them without a secret or selfish agenda.
- Knowledge (or understanding) means knowing someone in a personal way. I love how one scholar put it, "This is not 'knowledge-as-instrument' but 'knowledge' as a person shaper."[7] Paul's relationship with the Corinthians that was intuitive and personal.
- Patience is the Greek word *makroythmia*. It's a people-oriented patience. It can mean slowness in avenging wrongs, biting your tongue, or being calm while waiting to see how things end up. It also means enduring with people who can be difficult to love.
- Kindness can mean moral goodness in action. While patience is reactive, kindness is proactive. It is often related to helpfulness, actions or words that benefit others, or having a generous spirit.

This morning I confessed to the Lord the lack of some of these virtues in my life while dealing with some difficult situations. Let me put it this way: I find demonstrating purity, understanding, patience, and kindness an absolute breeze with the people I like. It's all those other people who cause these virtues to get jammed up. The critics Paul wrote to were those other people, and still he responded in Christlikeness. But how?

List four means or methods Paul used (vv. 6b-7).
1.

2.

3.

4.

When people sin against us or someone we love, when they're critical or emotionally unavailable, when they betray or unfairly accuse, we need something far more than a mere list of virtues to imitate. We need to respond in the Holy Spirit (John 14:26), in sincere love (2 Cor. 5:14), in truthful speech (Eph. 4:15), in the power of God (Eph. 1:18-19).

I know many of you are in the midst of difficult situations. People close to you are pushing the limits of your capacity for goodness. You're just trying to keep the peace—forget about adding virtues into the mix. The reality is neither Paul, nor we, can experience or express purity, knowledge, patience, and kindness without supernatural help.

When we consider living out biblical themes such as sacrificial love, turning the other cheek, and displaying godly virtues to difficult people, we can mistakenly believe we will become weak, needy people. We need to remember that righteousness is anything but weak and can be used as a weapon for good. Oh, yes, it is humble, kind, and long-suffering, but the righteousness of Christ is also strong and capable of repelling evil (Eph. 6:11-13). The point being, sometimes in our painful and difficult relationships we need to get in there with some spiritual weapons and fight.

Pray that God will instill the virtues we've discussed today in your heart and in your life.

DAY 5
Unequally Yoked *(2 Cor. 6:11-7:1)*

Today's reading begins with a straightforward plea for earnest relationship. Take a moment to quiet your heart before the Lord, asking Him to reveal His Word to you today.

Read 2 Corinthians 6:11-13.

Speaking freely, opening our hearts wide, and not withholding our affections, looks like a recipe for pain. If I make myself this vulnerable in a relationship, I throw open a window that someone I love could slam down on my fingers. Isn't it safer to protect, wall off, and batten down our hearts to the winds of rejection and betrayal? Safer, maybe. But this isn't the way of love. Or fullness of life. Or authentic community.

Make no mistake, Paul begged for a two-way street in relationship, but he couldn't force it into being. He pleaded for a return of affection from the Corinthians, but he couldn't control the outcome.

The next section can seem abrupt. But if we keep in mind Paul's desire for pure affection, I think the following verses fit snugly.

Read 2 Corinthians 6:14-7:1.

Yoke: "a wooden bar or frame by which two draft animals (as oxen) are joined at the heads or necks for working together."[8]

We can pretty much divide humanity into two segments: those who grew up in the church being taught about what it means to be "unequally yoked" and those who didn't. If you're part of the first group, you probably remember summer camps where this passage was used to drive home one point and one point only: Don't date non-Christians. If you're in the second group, you're wondering if this is a new way to do eggs. Suffice it to say, I hope we can have at least a little fun today. It's the last homework day of the session and you've earned it.

Let's begin by defining the term *yoke*, so we're all on the same page (your version may say "mismatched"). See margin. In Deuteronomy 22:10, the law prohibited a person to plow with a calf and a donkey together, as the calf was considered clean and the donkey unclean. Also, these mismatched animals would pull the yoke in different ways and with differing force.

Personal Response: Why do you think having a binding intimate relationship with an unbeliever is incompatible? Record your response in your journal.

Look at the following comparisons and fill in the missing blanks from verses 14-16. (I've given you the NIV translation, but feel free to use the words in your own translation.)

• What do righteousness and wickedness have in _____?
• What_____ can light have with darkness?
• What _____ is there between Christ and Belial?
• What does a believer and unbeliever have in _____?
• What _____ is there between the temple of God and idols?

If you're attached to someone in a double harness and your passions differ, worldviews clash, values aren't in sync, destinations are in different locations, then how in the world is this going to work? On the other hand, we've seen Paul clearly preach reconciliation to a lost world, so he certainly doesn't mean we shouldn't have relationships with unbelievers. Let's keep going. I think things will become clearer.

Back to 2 Corinthians 6:16, Paul said that we are the temple of the living God. This verse has major implications for our relationships. What are they?

Paul quoted several Old Testament passages here, weaving them together into a call for holiness. In verse 17, Paul quoted from the prophet Isaiah, who proclaimed freedom for the Israelites from the pagan city of Babylon.

Read about God's deliverance of his people in Isaiah 52:9-11.

Describe the excitement and hope of the setting.

Personal Reflection: When it comes to your being separate from what the world desires and prizes, do you look at it as a burden or a joy? Explain.

Summarizing this string of Old Testament references, Paul provided a reminder of Israel's history that has flowed into our present. God no longer dwells in temples made by hands, but in our hearts! He lives among us, and we are His people.

As a result of these promises, what are we urged to do in verse 7:1?

The verses from 2 Corinthians 6:11—7:1 are often framed in a way that highlights the negative: Don't be unequally yoked, don't touch

"Do not be yoked together with unbelievers. For what do righteousness and wickedness have in common? Or what fellowship can light have with darkness? What harmony is there between Christ and Belial? Or what does a believer have in common with an unbeliever? What agreement is there between the temple of God and idols?"
2 Corinthians 5:14—16a

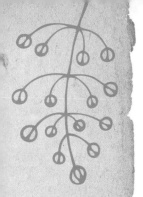

anything unclean, don't get contaminated by all that sin out there, come away (from all the fun). While some clear "negatives" are present, the context is entirely positive. We can't miss the love and relationship here!

We are the sons and daughters of God (2 Sam. 7:14), and He is a father to us. God longs to dwell with us right here in the middle of our earthly lives, walk beside us in our day-to-day lives, tend to us as a loving Father tends His beloved daughters. Do you see how this changes everything about the way we view the concept of being unequally yoked? Suddenly, we're not talking about staying separate from the world because Christians can never have fun (I mean our team motto is the word *no*, right?). Instead, this is a cry to separate ourselves from anything that might hinder our knowing and being known in Christ. It's for the sake of our freedom. In holiness we've been set apart. Do we really want to risk that honor by contaminating our bodies and spirits through a wrong relationship? Do we want to bind the freedom of our relationship with Christ because we're deeply bound to an unbeliever?

Your gut answer in this moment may be a swirl of yeses and noes. I surely understand this. For anyone who's desired a consequential relationship with someone who doesn't share your faith in Jesus, this can be a painful prospect. We've all longed for what this world has to offer while resisting the real life Jesus longs to give us. However, there is simply no unclean thing worth touching at the expense of holding the blessings the Father longs to give you. No binding relationship with an unbeliever is worth compromising unveiled intimacy with Jesus. No title or position rivals the title of daughter of the Lord Almighty.

You've accomplished so much this week. You've considered what it means to be truly home, whether on earth or in heaven. You've thought about the emphasis you put on your body and how one day that body will be swallowed up with an incorruptible one. You've been reminded that how you live on this earth matters, what it means to be reconciled to God, and what it means to be a messenger of that reconciliation to a weary world that so longs for it. You've also been encouraged to stretch your hearts open just a little wider, even if what you most want to do is self-protect; Love does not withhold. And finally, you've been refreshed by the loving heart behind God's command for us not to be unequally yoked with unbelievers.

THE NEW HAS COME

2 Corinthians 7:2–8:24

My five year-old nephew, Will, and my three year-old niece, Harper, were staying with me for the day. My brother dropped them off at eight in the morning and would pick them up after work at five—I was tired by approximately 9:42 a.m. This is simply due to the fact that I'm not used to answering a million questions before breakfast. Which brings me to breakfast. It's shocking the energy necessary for toasting blueberry waffles, cutting them into non-chokable sized pieces, dousing them with enough syrup to be visible to the toddler's eye while accounting for absorption— because once it soaks in, they don't buy that it's actually there. There's a science to all this.

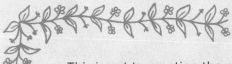

This is not to mention the remarkable brain power needed for choosing the appropriately colored cups for the right child. I've learned that yellow, pink, green, and blue cups can be interchanged at your whim until the day they catch onto color, at which point your life is officially over. The who-gets-what-colored-cup conversation is a universal one that cannot be solved by simply assigning each child his or her favorite color. Why? Because their favorite colors change without notice. We do not have the expertise to crack this code. It's a dynamic, complex formula that only they know and can use to torture us.

I hustled Will off to school and before I knew it, the time came for Harper and I to pick him back up. Time flies when they're gone. He no sooner had nestled into his car seat when he pulled three Chinese coins out of his pocket, coins his teacher had given him. They were colorful, sparkly little things—otherwise known as kindling logs for the argument that was about to catch fire in the backseat of the car. Will flashing his coins around was perfectly confusing for Harper, who isn't in school yet and didn't get to take home money. I tried to downplay the whole thing. "Harps, this is fake money," I explained, "You can't buy anything with those silly coins." This did little to deter her as Will clinked them, inspected them, tilted them so as to reflect and refract the rays of sun bearing through the car window. One of them was even pink—if Will didn't give Harper one of those coins she was going to sever her car seat harness with her teeth and rip them out of his stubby little fingers.

When you're trying to keep a moving vehicle on the road, it's difficult to get into deep discussions with preschoolers about sharing. The concept of enjoying something that is yours while realizing that it's only yours because it's been given to you, or you were graced with the power to earn it, is somewhat hard to understand. Whether you're four or forty, it is difficult to grasp this and come to the conclusion that your reasonable act of service is to share your fake coins (and your real ones).

We know inherently as believers that everything we have has been given to us by the Lord. Our homes, health, clothes, food, animals, spending cash, the chairs we sit on, the beds we curl up in, and the schools we attend all come from Him. Every possession is a gift. Our parents may have worked hard for it, but it's still a gift because God gives us the opportunity and power to work. We may have made a wise decision, but it is still a gift because God gives us the wisdom and wit to grow our money. So, the question is, what are we doing with the gifts God has given us? How are we using our resources for His Kingdom?

With what passion are we making everlasting deposits by spending ourselves to nourish hungry bodies, mend aching hearts, and propel the gospel to the ends of the earth? And doing all this with the blessings God has given us in the first place?

Out of the 13 chapters Paul wrote to the Corinthians, two of them are about the grace, joy, and privilege of generosity. I use these three words purposefully because these are the words Paul used. And they are so different from the words we normally think of when it comes to giving—words like sacrifice, duty, and misery. Later this week and at the start of next we'll study a scenario that involves a poor Gentile church in Macedonia, a poor Jewish church in Jerusalem, and the rather affluent church in Corinth we've come to know.

I won't give away the details, but what I want you to notice is the excitement that comes when we choose obedience through generosity. When we sacrificially give for Kingdom purposes, we get to know the heart of God, we more deeply attach to the people we're called to care for, we move out into deeper waters of faith and grace, and we share in the privilege of being part of something far more compelling than what money can buy. We'll notice that Paul and Titus (and God Himself—2 Cor. 8:16) were bursting with excitement over the financial blessing that they couldn't wait for the Jerusalem church to receive. But with equal zeal they couldn't wait for the blessing the Corinthian church would receive as a result of being the ones to supply that blessing to the church at Jerusalem.

Fly forward nearly two thousand years and God's heart is still beating for the poor, the lost, the wounded, the orphan, and the widow. He's still desperate for us to step out in faith and give beyond what we think we can, because we've been given a grace to do so. It's a privilege to be a participant in His work—it's where the joy is— and everything we have has been given to us.

On the way home from Will's preschool that afternoon, I witnessed the sprouting seeds of what God was already cultivating in his heart. "Here ya go, Harper," he said while handing her the coin with a bit of a smile, "you can have it." And there was joy all the way home.

Group Guide (Week 4)

Prepare
Spend some time in prayer, reflecting on what God has taught you so far and asking Him to continue to help you understand and see His Word clearly during the rest of your study of 2 Corinthians.

Review & Discuss
Review your homework and what you learned in Session 3 before you meet with your group, then read the introduction to Session 4 on the previous pages and highlight anything that you think is significant and anything you thought about relevant to 2 Corinthians that you might want to share with the group.

Given that Paul compared our bodies to tents, I want you to do a quick inventory of how much time, energy, and money you put into your physical body. This includes thinking about body image, clothes and makeup, shopping, browsing fashion websites and blogs, working out, getting manicures and pedicures, and hair cuts and colors. These are not bad things and there's not a right or wrong answer here. I want you to underline what three things listed above take up the bulk of your focus, then briefly explain why those three are most important to you. Did the results of your inventory surprise you? Convict you? Explain.

How has the Holy Spirit acted as a deposit of God's future redemption in your life? Think of specific instances where you knew beyond a shadow of a doubt He was with you and living inside you.

In Day 3, you learned a great deal about reconciliation, but let's explore it a little further by looking up several different other places in the New Testament where the word *reconcile* is used.

Look up the references below and discuss what each says about reconciliation.

Romans 5:10-11
1 Corinthians 7:10-11
Colossians 1:19-22
2 Corinthians 5:19

I hope you have a clearer and more meaningful picture of the word, *reconcile*. I may be most thankful for the peace reconciliation brings. You may have noted peace as one of the blessings mentioned in Colossians 1:20, a result of Christ's shed blood for our sin on the cross. Reconciliation always brings peace.

Looking back at Day 3, how is Jesus the only one who can make reconciliation with God possible?

You've studied five chapters worth of information on the church at Corinth. In what ways do you think the Corinthians may have been receiving God's grace in vain?

While I believe all the virtues of Christ are interconnected, which one of these four virtues on page 64 comes most naturally for you? Explain. Which one do you need to grow in?

Journal

When you think of all that the word "home" means to you, how much does the presence of Jesus factor into that? In other words, is He your ultimate sense of security? Is He your hope in trials? Is He the One you can't wait to thank in blessing? Do you run to Him first in times of anxiety? Journal your thoughts.

Take Action

As you approach Session 5 on giving and generosity, pray for God to prepare your heart for what's ahead and to open your eyes to how you can be a wise steward of all that He has given you. Not only material things, but begin to consider how God might have you give of your time to serve and help a friend or elderly neighbor.

- **Memorize:** 2 Corinthians 8:9
  Think on this verse as you go for a walk somewhere quiet. Then, thank God for sending His Son to become poor so that we might be rich in Him.

DAY 1
Wisdom for Relationships *(2 Cor. 7:2-10)*

In case you've lost track, you've completed three sessions of homework and journeyed through six chapters and one verse of 2 Corinthians. Do you know what this means? It means you can absolutely finish! Maybe you've sacrificed a bit of sleep or a few television shows to get here. You've laid aside a hobby or stayed up later at night. What I know is that you've made this happen. You've planned for it and protected it. And don't get down on yourself if not every question has been answered—we're showing up for intimacy with Jesus and life change, not good grades.

What I've found about sticking with a Bible study and being committed to a weekly gathering is that discipline usually ends up leading to desire. While a sense of duty may cause me to begin a study, somewhere in the process a change takes place and duty becomes delight. So keep at it. If discipline hasn't quite turned into desire just give it a little more time. And certainly pray for it. The Lord loves to give this to us.

Read 2 Corinthians 7:2-4.

In case you forgot how desperately Paul longed for relationship with the church at Corinth, he was still on that bandwagon. You may have thought all the pleading and longing wrapped with chapter 6, but surprise—Paul had more love. How was that even possible?

What did Paul say he had in the Corinthians (v. 4a)?

Biblically speaking, pride isn't normally a positive attribute, but in this case we get to go for it! We do well to take pride in another person who's growing in Christ. It's good to show our confidence in those we've poured into. I take pride in the girls I disciple when I see them making decisions that please the Lord. I have a ton of confidence in my parents who have had a faithful run of ministry. I'm overjoyed when I see my young nieces and nephews tottering out on faith. I want to be better at expressing my enthusiasm for the progress of other believers.

I appreciate Paul's wisdom here. He boosted the Corinthians in all the ways he could genuinely be proud of them, meanwhile not avoiding the areas that needed addressing.

You may be wondering why Paul suddenly talked about his pride in the Corinthians, his confidence in them, the encouragement he had because of them. Not for nothing but they had been a little disappointing. They bought into the false teachers, accused Paul of being a fraud, and cozied up a little too close with the unbelievers in Corinth. So what was going on? Why the change of attitude? Part of it had to do with the way Paul laid out his letter. Let me show you.

You'll remember from earlier in our study Paul's explanation for changing his travel plans to visit the Corinthians. In the middle of that explanation, he took an approximate five chapter hiatus to discuss the nature of true Christian ministry (2:14-7:4). The Corinthians had been looking for someone with worldly credentials such as wealth, notoriety, and status. Paul responded that his was a humble ministry all about hearts, led by the Spirit, housed in fragile vessels, not about himself but about Jesus, focused on eternity instead of the temporal, grounded in reconciliation, and often characterized by suffering.

For the sake of continuity, read 2 Cor. 2:12-13, picking up with 2 Cor 7:5-7. How did God bring comfort to Paul?

There is no comfort quite like the comfort of God that comes through a friend. In Paul's case, it was the comfort of God, from the Corinthians, that came through Titus—the comfort train chugging from Corinth to Macedonia. If we were handing out Oscars for 2 Corinthians, the movie, Titus would win "Best Supporting Actor" hands down. Since he would make several more appearances, let's do some quick research on him.

Read Galatians 2:1-3. What nationality was Titus and what did he do alongside Paul?

Read Titus 1:4. Keeping in mind that Paul was a circumcised Jew, how did he refer to Titus?

This may not seem like a big deal today, but the fact that Titus was an uncircumcised Greek and one of Paul's spiritual sons is a transformational demonstration of the gospel. Circumcised Jews wouldn't have had anything to do with uncircumcised Gentiles before Christ. But when Jesus came, He tore down the dividing wall between Jews and Gentiles (Eph. 2:11-22), offering salvation to all nations, tribes, and tongues (Col. 3:11). Paul, a Jew of all Jews, considered Titus not only a close partner in ministry but his very son.

Read 2 Corinthians 7:7. List everything the Corinthians expressed to Titus about Paul. What did this lead Paul to?

"Often a wise leader knows how to blend words of confrontation with words of encouragement."

Continue reading 2 Corinthians 7:8-10.

The letter Paul referred to is the one we read about in 2 Corinthians 2:4. Remember he decided to write the Corinthians a letter instead of making another painful visit to them. Sometimes conflict needs to be resolved in person, other times the situation is so raw that sending a message is the wisest move. Biblical examples support both. And sometimes there's just no way to know what's right, apart from the leading of the Holy Spirit.

Much like Paul's conflicting feelings in verse 8, our godly decisions don't always lead to tidy emotions. In one sense, Paul didn't regret the painful letter because he finally knew it had helped the Corinthians, but in the agonizing in-between stages he'd grieved over it. The reason Paul could release his regret was that the sorrow caused by the letter led to the church's repentance. This word *repentance* literally means to change your mind or to turn around.

Godly sorrow leads to _____.
Worldly sorrow leads to _____.

Personal Response: Think of a time when you were sorry about something only because of what it cost you: exposure, shame, loss of relationship or freedom. Did you experience worldly sorrow or godly sorrow?

Now, consider a time when your sorrow over your sin led you to seek God's forgiveness and change your ways.

Wordly sorrow or godly sorrow? Briefly explain the difference between the two.

Godly sorrow leads us to repentance, but so does something else. What is it according to Romans 2:4?

A friend pointed out that not only does godly sorrow lead to repentance, it also leads to intimacy. When we're truly sorry for our sin, we return to a walk of obedience to Christ and a new level of intimacy is established. Take heart if you're experiencing the grief of godly sorrow, for this leads to repentance. Then, once you reach repentance, you'll continue onto salvation.

DAY 2
The Good of Godly Sorrow *(2 Cor. 7:11-16)*

Have you ever been alarmed at how little you know yourself?

Why did I respond like that? From where did this roller coaster of emotions come sweeping in? What's this conflict I'm feeling?

It's a strange phenomenon that our familiar selves can occasionally feel like people we've never met. Sometimes we need a rocky path to jostle the confusion free, a godly sorrow to expose our true hearts. I wish there was an easier way to reach the true core of our beings, but the encouraging news from today's text is that godly sorrow not only exposes who we really are, but also produces change. Results. An actual difference. Like, we're not who we used to be. When we experience the sorrow God intends (2 Cor. 7:9), the impurities fall away and we emerge anew. I think you're going to love today's Word.

Read 2 Corinthians 7:11-12.

The painful letter Paul wrote to the Corinthians had been received in the best possible way. They didn't fight back, become defensive, spread gossip, or ditch the faith. They'd messed up, but Paul's point wasn't to focus on their wrongs, instead he longed for them to respond and be restored. And they'd done both.

Let's look more intently at each of their positive responses.
1. The Corinthians were stirred out of passivity and complacency, becoming earnest and diligent in what really mattered.
2. The desire they had to clear themselves didn't mean they hadn't done anything wrong. Instead, it was an eager desire to explain their actions, admitting guilt where needed.
3. The outrage they expressed could be anger at the person who sinned mentioned in chapter 2, the false prophets who had been slandering Paul, or even themselves for being complacent while all this was going on.
4. They had a newly awakened alarm/fear. This word could mean awe-inspired reverence for God, or a sobering respect in relation to a person, perhaps Paul.
5. The deep longing or desire was an "intense positive interest in something,... Marked by a sense of dedication."[2] The church at Corinth had a new longing for Paul and his friends that hadn't been present before.
6. They also had a special concern/zeal/enthusiasm for Paul and the things of the Lord.

7. And lastly, all this led to justice. Some translations say vindication or punishment, but in this list of all positive and heart-warming descriptions, justice seems best. Specifically, this could relate to the punishment of the offender (2 Cor. 2:5-11), or generally, a commitment to deal with sin correctly and lovingly.

Personal Reflection: Review the previous list. Which of the seven have you experienced as a result of the Lord taking you through a season of godly sorrow? In other words, how has your repentance led you to similar responses?

For me, the most significant season of repentance in my life led to a deeper desire to esteem obedience in a culture that blurs right and wrong. I became more concerned about holiness in my life and in those I serve. The words Paul used in verse 11 are words of passion and feeling—there's not a bland description in the bunch. I believe the more repentant we are, the more passionate we become for righteousness and goodness.

According to verse 11, what had the Corinthians shown or proven themselves to be?

The Corinthians were innocent, pure, clear. Yes, they had sinned but they had made things right, thus they could be called clean. This is such a testament to how God takes the shame, guilt, and record of our past and restores us to innocence.

Read Colossians 1:21-22. What makes us pure and blameless?

The Corinthians' hearts had been revealed and their motives disclosed. They'd aligned themselves with truth and wanted to act in accordance with that truth. But the path getting there hadn't been easy for either side. Paul had been misunderstood and wounded, and we can be sure a ton of feelings had been battered. The Corinthians didn't understand why Paul had seemingly stood them up. I can only imagine the gossip grapevine flying through town, false teachers luring people away in the church's hour of weakness, and people taking sides down the middle of the sanctuary. Thankfully, Titus stepped in as the messenger and peacemaker. This was a peak time to be a Christian counselor. This is church work, and how this was resolved is church work at its best.

Turn back to Deuteronomy 8:2. Why did God allow the Israelites to endure the wilderness? How is this similar to what came from the Corinthians' experience?

Let's close our day by returning to 2 Corinthians. Read verses 7:13-16.

Try to picture the day Titus came to Macedonia and found Paul, the two of them reunited for the first time in months. Imagine Paul's anxiety having reached its crest after wondering and agonizing over how his beloved church in Corinth had responded to the painful corrective letter. *Did they hate him? Had the church blown up? Had God's work in Corinth been lost?* And then envision Titus, after having embraced Paul, saying, "It's all good, Paul. It's so, so good. They're doing great! They understand they've messed up, and they're really sorry. And not just sorry for being caught, but truly sorry before the Lord. They heard you, and they've made changes—heart changes. Oh, and they're dying to see you, Paul— they're just dying to see you!"

Christian relationships are not easy, but they're worth it. We're simply not meant to tread through life alone—without someone to douse our souls with refreshment, without a bunch of fellow sojourners to brag about because we're just so proud of their obedience to the Lord. We're not meant to exist without this band known as the church, and in this church we're doubly blessed if we find ourselves a Titus or two. These are the ones we achingly miss when they are absent (2 Cor. 2:13). They're the ones who tell us the truth and expect truth from us, partly because they already know it. They stand in the gap for us, helping us in unpleasant tasks. They're willing to do the hard stuff for us because they love us and they love the body of Christ.

> **Personal Response: Close today by thanking God for the dear friends He's given you. Pray that you can be a Titus to them and they to you.**

DAY 3
The Privilege of Generosity *(2 Cor. 8:1-9)*

I'm so excited to explore chapters 8-9 with you over the next few days. These chapters will take us to an area of our Christian lives where we struggle to give God control. Call it your purse, wallet, hipster leather bag, whatever, He wants in. Actually He wants us to dig in there ourselves and cheerfully—and I do mean with some serious happiness—offer Him our resources, particularly for those in need. Before you start reading today's text, ask the Lord to open your mind to receive and apply whatever He's going to put on your heart in the next few days.

Some background for today's reading: The Macedonian churches mentioned in this chapter included the churches at Philippi, Thessalonica, and Berea. These churches were extremely poor and in the middle of a significant trial. Still, they were eager to give to the Jewish believers who were also living in extreme poverty.

Read 2 Corinthians 8:1-9.

> **What two seemingly opposite things resulted in rich generosity (v. 2)?**
>
> **Personal Response: How do you think it's possible for seemingly opposites like joy and poverty to overflow into generosity? (Note: This is not just giving of money, but also of our time.)**

Occasionally, as I read the Bible, a single word will hit me. One word in the middle of sentences, narrative, punctuations, theological truths, will wave its arms and say, "Look at me, Kel." This happened when I reached verse four. It's the word *privilege*, which may or may not be the word your translation uses, although the message is the same. The Greek word is a beautiful one, *charis*. It can mean grace, benefit, favor, or delight. This deeply impoverished Macedonian church, made up of Gentiles, had a deep desire to give to the Jewish believers in Jerusalem. They didn't look at it as a chore, duty, or hardship, rather they saw it as a privilege! As if they had the inside scoop on how to get into this special deal of giving even more away to their Jewish brothers and sisters.

> **Personal Reflection: Put a mark on the spectrum below that represents how you look at monetary giving.**

> Avoid   Eager
>
> |---|

Some of us want to hold onto our money because we love to save. This is me. I don't want to be caught unprepared, so I like being able to turn some money into more money by putting it in places where it can grow. Others like having money so they can spend it. We want the ability to acquire cars, clothes, tickets, and other pleasures. Regardless of why you like to have money—to save or to spend—it can be problematic if it becomes your ultimate reliance or happiness. As much as I love to *put* money away, the Lord has opened my heart to the joy and privilege of *giving* it away. This desire is not natural to me, not something I was born with. In fact, Paul revealed very specifically how this desire comes about in our lives.

Look at verses 8:1 and 7. What had God given the Macedonians that enabled them to give so generously?

According to verse 6, Titus was the one who went to Corinth to help coordinate this collection for the poor in Jerusalem. The Corinthians had apparently started this act of giving (1 Cor. 16:1-4), but what was Titus there to ensure?

Read verse 7. List the five areas Paul acknowledged that the Corinthians excelled in, followed by a sixth quality he wanted to make sure they didn't forget:

1.

2.

3.

4. *Earnestness*

5. *Love*

6.

Paul commended the Corinthians for succeeding in several areas, but wanted to make sure they didn't forget generous giving in the process. This tells me that you can love the Lord and excel in certain Christ-like qualities and still miss the vital grace of generosity. As we make our way through chapters 8-9, we're going to record eleven truths about generosity. This will help us reframe the act of sacrificial giving from something we resist to one of the great privileges of our lives. Today, we'll record the first two. After circling the correct word, write these truths on page 112.

1. *God's definition of generous giving isn't dependent on how much or how little* (peace, health, wealth, joy) *a person has (8:2,12).*

2. The experience of giving is a privilege that's accompanied by (peace, health, wealth, joy) even in difficult circumstances (8:2).

Personal Response: Why do you think Paul didn't command the Corinthians to give? (See v. 8. Also, look ahead at 9:7.)

I'm always inspired by other believers who genuinely model the character of Christ. When Paul shared that the Macedonians were begging him for the privilege to give to the Jewish believers in Jerusalem, he was holding them up as a model for the Corinthians. The Macedonians were giving out of joy, not duty. Paul wanted the Corinthians to experience the same privilege and joy in their giving.

Other people can inspire us in great ways, but none like the person of Jesus. Write out 2 Corinthians 8:9 in the margin.

Here's a truth that has recently convicted my heart: I have become less "rich" for people, but I have yet to become poor for anyone. It is one thing for me to skim off the top of my abundance, another thing to scrape off a layer of my pleasures or savings, but it's something entirely different altogether to get down to the foundation of all I have and give it to someone else that they might become rich. This is the way of Jesus. He was rich in that He shared in the privileges of equality with God (Phil. 2:6), the fullness of unbroken fellowship with The Father and Holy Spirit. He became poor by taking on our flesh, confining Himself to the limitations and suffering of this world, ultimately dying on a cross. And He did it to make us rich. Oh, dear girls, not rich in material stuff, because this can actually make us poor in matters of the spirit. But rich in peace that doesn't cut and run in the face of uncertainty. Rich in contentment that knows how to ride both the waves of abundance and trying times. Rich in intimacy with Him that oddly enough grows deeper and more precious in suffering's soil. Rich in joy whether by the gifts of material blessings that bring us a measure of happiness, or the joy that comes with giving our lives away. Rich in life—abundant and eternal.

Earlier today we looked at a word found in verses 1 and 7, and now we see it again in verse 9. What was behind Jesus' giving up of His riches and becoming poor for us?

Our ability to be generous and to give sacrificially give is directly related to God's grace. Ask the Lord for more grace in your giving. Ask Him for the opportunity to share in the privilege of coming alongside others with the gift of generosity. It's where the joy is.

DAY 4
The Heart of Giving *(2 Cor. 8:10-15)*

On a scale of one to ten, how excited are you to give money to your church, a ministry, or the poor? What if I told you that for the rest of your life you'd have enough money to buy everything you want, travel everywhere you want, save as much as you want, and anything you gave away would be on top of your limitless supply of money, now how excited would you be to give? In other words, if giving didn't actually require you to sacrifice in any way, would you be more excited to give your babysitting money or set aside that tithe?

The reason I ask this question is that when challenged to give, we may be reluctant because of what giving will cost us. If I give $10 a month to help sponsor a child, that's $10 less I have for going to the movies. If I tithe 10 percent of my income to my church, there goes my gas money. If I make that one-time donation to a house for orphans, I don't see how I'll be able to go on a trip with my youth group. Bottom line, what makes giving so difficult is that when we give our money away we're giving up what that money can do for us.

You've probably heard people say things like, *Man, I wish I were independently wealthy so I could just give money away to people in need.* This assumes three things that I don't think are true: First, if we were independently wealthy we'd automatically give tons of money away. Second, we need to be financially set before we can give as freely as we want. Third, the higher the amount of money we give, the more pleased God is with our giving. In today's passage, Paul dismantled these assumptions as he encouraged the Corinthians to give to the church in Jerusalem with passion and excitement.

Read 2 Corinthians 8:10-15.

In verse 10, what motivated the Corinthians to give?

Duty   A Command   Desire   Prayer

Personal Response: Why do you think Paul needed to remind them to complete the process of giving? I mean, if they had the desire to give wouldn't that naturally lead to fulfilling the gift?

Personal Reflection: What causes a disconnect between your willingness to give and actually following through (*laziness, fear of the future, selfishness, etc.*)?

Re-read verses 8:13-15, and jot down a summary sentence of the basic message.

In verse 15, Paul quoted from the book of Exodus about God's provision for the Israelites during their wilderness wanderings. Read Exodus 16:11-18 to get a better understanding of what Paul was talking about.

Ultimately, how much did the people gather (v. 18)?

The Lord's provision of manna for the Israelites was a gift and also a test—He wanted to see if they would obediently trust Him by not hoarding the manna overnight (except on the sixth day). The Lord had promised to consistently provide, day by day. The church at Corinth had a great deal more wealth and resources than the impoverished Jews in Jerusalem. It wouldn't be right for them to hoard that wealth, stuff more rooms full of furniture, or sail on extravagant vacations while their brothers and sisters could barely put food on the table. The Gentile Corinthians had; the Jerusalem Jews had not. Or is that totally accurate? Look again at verse 14.

After the Corinthians supplied the need of the Jews, what would in turn happen?

Personal Reflection: If the Corinthians were fairly well off and the Jews were significantly impoverished, what need would the Corinthians have and how could the Jews supply for that need? Give this some thought.

There are possibly two thoughts with this passage. One, practically speaking, there could come a time in the future when the economic tables would be turned. The Corinthian church could be in want and the Jerusalem church would financially provide for them. Theologically speaking, the Jews, special in God's sight as His chosen people, had already given to the Gentiles in the sense that their spiritual riches had been shared with them—actually with all of us.

In a few days, I'll be leaving for the Amazon in Brazil for Justice & Mercy International's Fifth Annual Jungle Pastor's Conference. The one-hundred pastors and wives I'll spend the week with are, by our standards, immensely poor. Most live in huts, gather their own food, sleep in hammocks, and live on less than $100 month. But make no mistake, they will supply my need out of their abundance. They will melt my religious skepticism with the fire of their faith. The fullness of joy they have in knowing Jesus will inspire me to long for Him with more fervor. The way God is using them to spread the gospel down the Amazon will cast light on the silly, petty, flimsy things on which I spend energy. They will expose the needs I have outside of what my bank account can supply. I will supply their want and they mine. This is equality.

Personal Reflection: Describe how an experience of sacrificial giving ended up supplying a need for you.

We've learned three more concepts about giving to add to your list. See as follows. Jot them down on page 112 of the Session 6 Group Guide.

3. *Our willingness to give must be matched with actual follow-through (8:11).*

4. *God cares more about our desire to give than the amount we're able to give (8:12). (See Mark 12:41-44.)*

5. *The discipline of giving is for the mutual benefit of the giver and the receiver (8:14).*

Personal Response: Which of these three truths is the most eye-opening to you, and how will it affect your giving?

I can't tell you how many times I've wanted to give to a ministry or tithe to my church, but let the moment pass me by. It's the strangest thing that somehow I can get all my credit card information entered online before the one-day sale ends for that purse, but I can put off sending that check into my church. I won't forget to bring my gift card to the nail salon, but I'll forget to bring money to church for my tithe. Anyone else? Anyone?

I'm hoping we've allowed the Holy Spirit to change our view of giving so we'll see it as a privilege as opposed to a duty, that our hearts would long to be generous. Giving is a gateway to joy. And when we see it through this lens my prayer for us is that we'll find ourselves wanting to give as eagerly as we used to want to save or spend.

DAY 5
In This Together *(2 Cor. 8:16-24)*

We really are in this together. No one can save the world alone. Whether we're helping organize a fundraiser, fighting human trafficking, building a church in a developing country, or being sent as on a mission trip—we need each other. We need the assortment of gifts the Lord has given each of us working together. We also need accountability, the friend to keep us in check and ensure that when success transpires no one's head gets too big for the door. Any time money is involved, especially for charitable purposes, responsible people are essential for safeguarding and directing its use. We need one another for mutual encouragement when ministry results are slim and for prayer when we've run out of spunk. Some people will need to stay and manage the foundation while others will be called to go and pioneer new territory. No matter what piece God has given you to manage, be certain that your responsibility is essential to the whole and when you carry it out, you will not be alone.

Read 2 Corinthians 8:16-24.

Titus was eager, full of enthusiasm to run forward with this project. I have to admit I don't always have this passion for ministry. I want to desire others above myself and get more excited about someone coming to know Christ than I get over a new sofa. But too often our fleshly hearts beat for the things of the world, don't they? So how do we get the passion of a Paul, Titus or the unnamed brothers mentioned in this passage?

> **Verse 16 reminds me of a favorite passage from Nehemiah. Both texts give us a peek into the answer. Look up Nehemiah 2:11-12 and compare it to 2 Corinthians 8:16. From where does a passion to serve others come?**

I love that God gave Titus the same passion for the Corinthians that He'd given Paul. When God breaks our hearts and the hearts of our community for the same cause a shared passion is ignited. A bonfire of activity crackles and whistles and we bond around its warmth. We suddenly have ministry stuff to talk about that's more exciting than church gossip, more fulfilling than a marathon day of television. My mom just texted me a picture of herself and two of her girlfriends, Jean and Cheryl, putting together hand-sewn gift bags of makeup and beautifying products for the pastor's wives I'm about to see in the Amazon. Some stay, some go, some sew floral

bags and put lipstick in them, others deliver those bags. This is what we call teamwork.

> **Think of the people who share the same desire God's given you for the poor, lost, or hurting (or any people group, really). In the margin, list what you love most about sharing in ministry with them.**

> **Personal Response: In verse 17, Paul said that Titus responded to his request to travel to Corinth and oversee the collection of this offering for the Jews. Is there a current opportunity to be involved in a ministry that you've turned down for the wrong reasons? (Think selfishness, insecurity, pride, fear, etc.) Take a moment to lay this opportunity back before the Lord with a heart willing to be obedient to His call.**

Sharing responsibilities can be tough for leaders because we don't always want to hand over control. We have a specific way we do things. And what happens if we hand over control to someone who uses a different translation of the Bible or a different brand of computer? But notice that even the great apostle Paul entrusted ministry opportunities to others. He also needed capable, gifted people to step up around him.

> **You may not be in vocational ministry like Paul, but all of us are called to disciple others. Take a moment to ask the Lord to show you a Titus in your life that you can mentor and invest in.**

> **Two "brothers" were mentioned in this passage but they weren't given names. What was said about each of them (vv. 18-19,22)?**

Paul took great pains to avoid any criticism over the way this offering was administered (vv. 21-22). We all know that anytime a large sum of money is involved, people scrutinize and question how it's being handled. Knowing this, Paul not only made sure he was acting rightly in the Lord's eyes, but also in the eyes of _____ (v. 21).

> **As we close the week, I want you to reread verses 23-24. Why do you think Paul took the time to put an extra stamp of approval on Titus and these brothers?**

Throughout my years in the church I've seen the body of Christ work wonders like no other entity on earth. I've also seen—and shamefully admit been a part of—gossip, criticism, and critique of leadership. Pastors and church leaders need our encouragement. They need the benefit of the doubt sometimes. We need to cut them some slack. Remember, they're meeting a thousand needs at a time. And that sometimes when something looks like favoritism, or pride, or manipulation it may simply be that we're not seeing the whole picture.

Paul knew the Corinthians may not be accepting of Titus or these other brothers—they'd hardly been accepting of Paul himself. So he gently reminded them to show Titus and his friends the _____ of their love (circle below).

Intentions   Hope   Wisdom   Proof

Personal Response: As you think of your church's ministry leaders, what is one way you can show them the proof of your love this week? We can waste so much time talking about how things could be better or what the leadership isn't doing for us, but none of this amounts to anything profitable. Let's prove our love to our ministry leaders who serve us so tirelessly. They are literally, as Paul put it, the glory of Christ.

We now have two more truths about generosity to add to our list on page 112. Look back at verses 8:20-21.

6. Giving must be done in the right spirit and in the right way.

We've already noted that several churches were involved in this endeavor to help the church in Jerusalem. In addition to Paul, Titus and two other brothers were also helping.

7. A lifestyle of generosity is not an individual endeavor but a team effort (8:16-24).

I have a heart to see ministry accomplished, but I'm painfully aware of the areas I lack in to accomplish that ministry. This is one of the reasons I love teamwork in the body of Christ. I'm grateful to work with people whose skills, personalities, and spiritual gifts are different from mine. Not only do I cherish their friendships, but also they make up for my lack—and hopefully I theirs. The problem is that we're sometimes threatened by other people's strengths, especially in areas where we're weak. We may not understand people who are simply different from us, which can lead us to judge and steer clear of instead of appreciate and links arms with. So, at the close of this session's study, let's look to enjoy and embrace the gifts and personalities of others. Let's encourage each other and work together. We have a world that desperately needs Christ's body to serve in unity. Let's create space to serve as a team by laying aside our insecurities—a spiritually and physically hungry world will be so thankful we did.

SESSION 5

RETHINKING GENEROSITY

2 Corinthians 9:1–10:18

Aunthood is a bit like motherhood without the day-to-day responsibilities and college tuition bills. It's a little like being a grandmother but with a smidge more youth. For me, being an aunt has been a lovely surprise. Not the actual day it happened—I had nine months to anticipate the event—but the unexpected joy into which it has so wonderfully evolved.

Aunthood crept up on me.

These little creatures kept springing into the world, crawling into my house then strutting through the kitchen demanding juice boxes. Suddenly there were five of them. Actual humans. All with distinct personalities, angelic cheeks, and germs. Most of them are now in school, having flung me out there as a single branch on their kindergarten family trees—a precious bough I alone hold in each of their lives. They've given me a place and they've given me stories.

I remember when my youngest niece, Holland, was born. Her six-year-old sister's, Maryn's, excitement bubbled over with sisterly zeal. She was old enough to snuggle a real life doll who cooed and made smacking noises with her button mouth. Emmett, who was four at the time, was not nearly as amused. For him, visiting Holland in the hospital during those first few days was a real yawner.

At the same time, Emmett's parts of speech were in the throes of development. He routinely pluralized the pronoun "she" by making it "hers." As in, "Mom, hers is really bothering me." Or, "Mom, will you tell hers to stop." So, when Emmett was told the family was going to visit his newborn sister in the hospital for the second day in a row, his response was, "We have to go see *hers* again?"

When my sister, Katie, was released from the hospital, her husband, Brad, picked her and Holland up. Then, their newly enlarged family headed straight to school to collect Mary and Emmett. They skipped across the schoolyard, and Emmett punched the button that opens the side door to the minivan. Methodically, it slid open inch-by-inch, just like it always did, only this time newborn Holland was taking up a seat in the car. Emmett lamented with total shock, "You mean *hers* is still here?"

"Buddy, get in the car," Brad said, "*Hers* is going to be here for the rest of your life."

I've never forgotten this because most of us can relate. We've had that moment when we realize, for better or worse, we are stuck with a certain person or people or church congregation. Maybe it's the result of our own choosing or maybe it's what we discovered on the other side of the car door—the one we had no choice but to step through. None of us are exempt from having to get along with trying family members, working through complicated relationship triangles, or dealing with quirky church dynamics. We've all had that moment of realization that despite how tired and beat up we may be, *hers* is still here. And maybe *hers* is not going anywhere.

This is where the final few chapters of 2 Corinthians shoot into the sky with a bang. The difficult false teachers and confused church members of Corinth didn't seem to be going anywhere, and the attacks on Paul weren't ceasing. In the middle of a rather explosive environment, Paul stays with them. He continued to fight for the relationship. I keep thinking about these Corinthians and how my propensity would have been to clap the dust off my hands and move onto another city—to find a more grateful bunch of believers who would be happy to have someone like the apostle Paul as their spiritual father. Surely, other churches in other cities would have been more appreciative. But you know what it boiled down to? A calling.

During this session we'll see that Corinth was part of an assignment God had given Paul. It was smack in a sphere in which God had commissioned him to serve. Yes, Paul loved the Corinthians deeply, but the stamina of affection can only carry you so far. Sometimes the only thing keeping us in the race are the endorphins of pure calling. I don't know who you're called to care for, but my hunch is that a few of them may be wearing you out. Maybe you're not feeling appreciated, they seem disinterested, you fear you're being taken advantage of, or they keep slipping back into old patterns. This is when you press in, step up, push back, and stay engaged. Why? Because you've been called.

The relentless commitment that Paul demonstrated with the Corinthians is a trait I want more of. But this trait is shaped over the long haul, as we choose not to abandon a group of people just because things have become difficult. Or things aren't what they used to be. Or because *hers* is still here.

As we enter Session 5 together, I have a prayer for you: that Christ's love will compel you to stay committed in those trying relationships. When you're temped to draw harsh judgment from your sheath, instead draw humble authority, and use it to build up rather than tear down. I pray you won't lose the pure desire for people that can easily blur into desiring their possessions or what they can do for you. I pray the Holy Spirit gives you discernment to know when to be soft spoken and when to be bold, when to let an offense roll off your back and when to confront. As you fulfill the ministry assignment the Lord has given you, may you view the people in your spheres no longer from a human perspective, but as in Christ (2 Cor. 5:16-17). He can make even the most challenging person new. Even *hers*.

Group Guide (Week 5)

You're doing great, girls! Halfway to the finish line and our prayer is that you are learning more and more about Paul's letter to the church at Corinth. Isn't the church today more like the church at Corinth than you expected?

Prepare

Pray for the endurance to continue on strong in this Bible study. Review your homework and any notes from Week 4 and read the introduction for Session 5, as well as 2 Corinthians 9:1–10:18.

Review & Discuss

Skim through your homework from Session 4 and circle or highlight anything that stood out to you. Work through the following questions as a group, then share your responses either with the entire group, or break up with partners to share and pray together.

> One writer translated Paul's words in verse 3, "You are in my very heart, and you will be there in death and life alike."[1] Who has a place in your heart like no other? With whom would you live and die? Take some time to pray for these precious relationships—even if they're strained right now.

> What part of Paul's description of Christian ministry has been the most eye-opening to you? Explain.

> Not all conflicts work out like Paul's. However, I believe many can be resolved if we lovingly confront the situation like Paul did. Is there any relationship you need to fight for like Paul and Titus fought for the Corinthians? Spend some time praying, journaling, or reflecting with the Lord about this.

> List the seven results godly sorrow produced in the Corinthians (I filled in the first one for you).

1. *Earnestness or Diligence*

2.

3.

4.

5.

6.

7.

Look back at Day 3 of your homework. Think of a time when you were sorry about something only because of what it cost you: exposure, shame, or loss of relationship or freedom.

In what ways did Jesus become poor for us? In what ways have we been made rich because of Him? To better understand this, read Philippians 2:5-8.

Read 2 Corinthians 8:9 as many times as you need for it to settle into your heart. Do you take the grace of Jesus for granted or do you see His sacrificial gift as a privilege to model? Explain.

Journal

Take some time to consider the last discussion question in depth. Then, journal your thoughts. You'll continue to learn what true generosity according to the Letter of 2 Corinthians looks like in this week's homework.

Take Action

Write a note of encouragement and thanks to someone you take pride in. Open your heart wide to him or her. Be diligent as you continue to work through each session's homework. Start with Day 1 of the homework on the following page and commit to going through all five days, even if that means setting your alarm to get up earlier in the mornings.

- **Memorize**: 2 Corinthians 10:4-5
  Circle and underline key phrases and words to help memorize these verses. Read the verse aloud and work with a partner to commit to memorizing this verse together. Apply this to your lives as you seek to take ever thought captive in obedience to Christ (v. 5).

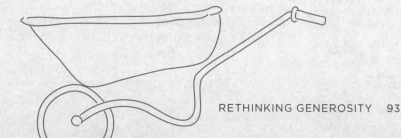

DAY 1
Held Accountable *(2 Cor. 9:1-5)*

When I step back from the details of 2 Corinthians, I see the letter as one resounding call to the adventure of a life of ministry. No believer is exempt. Every one of us has an assignment from the Lord to be by of Him. That concept, used by the Lord, is one I've known since childhood. But last week, while plodding up a hillside in Brazil with my friend Milton, whose first language is Portuguese, I heard it anew. His English is impeccable, but occasionally he misses a nuance by a thread, making the expression especially memorable. He was talking about what a blessing it is to be useful to God. And I heard the Lord in a new way: As believers, we're not simply used by Him, we're useful to Him. Our time, talents, resources, experience, education, personality, and heart—when surrendered to Him— become more than singular tools He uses. Rather, our whole beings become gloriously useful to Almighty God.

Dear sister, this has been one of the greatest privileges and honors of my life: to be useful in God's hands. When we choose to align ourselves with God and His ways, however imperfectly, He mysteriously gathers the darkest seasons and woeful failures of our past, transforms them and makes us, well, useful in His Kingdom. To God be the glory! I know what some of you are thinking: God doesn't need us. True, He is all-powerful and "is not served by human hands, as if He needed anything" (Acts 17:25). At the same time, in His sovereignty He has called us to be co-laborers with Him, given us spiritual gifts unique to each of us, and commanded us to tell everyone we know about the good news. Consider the unrivaled privilege of being useful to God.

I'm so excited to dive into Chapter 9 with you, which continues our emphasis on a lifestyle of generosity.

Read 2 Corinthians 9:1-5.

> **If the Corinthians were so eager to give, why did Paul send the brothers ahead of the collection?**

I've noticed a trend: People increasingly dislike being managed or answering to authority. More than ever, it seems, we esteem independence and the idea that we shouldn't have to answer to anyone. Never mind the truth that living outside of authority is actually not freedom at all. In the case of the Corinthians, Paul wanted to make sure they followed through on their plan to give. He didn't want to be ashamed of them or them be ashamed of themselves in front of the Macedonians. This meant the process needed oversight. The Corinthians needed accountability.

My friend pointed out that when Paul's friends visited Corinth, it wasn't to pressure them to give more, but to urge them to do what they said they would do. Their visit was a call to integrity and responsibility.

Personal Response: How open are you to being held accountable? Do you get defensive when people speak into your life or want to keep up with your progress?

Last week, we read about how the Macedonian church had inspired the church at Corinth to give to the Jerusalem church (2 Cor. 8:1-5). Then, it was the other way around: The generosity of Achaia (surrounding area of Corinth) had stirred up the Macedonian church with eagerness to give (v. 2).

Look back at 2 Corinthians 8:11. What needed to match the Corinthians' readiness or eagerness to give?

There's a difference between a readiness of intention and a readiness of completion.[2] I've had lots of great intentions over the years, but I've not always had the same resolve to bring that readiness to fulfillment. I can't tell you how many times I've left the Amazon thinking, *I need to learn Portuguese.* But life crowds out my intentions. We can hear an inspiring testimony at church and decide we want to give to that person's ministry, but by the time we drive home we've settled back into the demands of our lifestyle and bank accounts—the moment is lost. Or maybe we've been invited to give our time in an ongoing way. In the moment we're ready to go, but then homework and practice tug at our time and we pass up the opportunity to serve. Paul knew that the Corinthians—and we—needed help completing a task they were inspired to begin.

I'm encouraged by the detail given to the planning and administration of this large gift to the Jerusalem church. It makes me grateful for accountants, administrators, and those who love a spreadsheet. It helps me appreciate the ones who give their time to be overseers, like Titus and the brothers. Most of the time money doesn't appear, but has to be raised. And funds don't magically distribute themselves, they must be overseen. The church of Corinth had great intentions to give, but fulfilling those intentions required planning and accountability. We need the same structure for our giving.

Personal Reflection: According to 2 Corinthians 9:5, why do you think planning ahead for the collection would keep the gift from being given grudgingly?

For our eighth truth in our "11 Truths About Generosity," turn to page 112 and fill in this phrase as #8.

8. *A lifestyle of generous giving requires planning.*

Take a journey with me to another part of Scripture. Read Luke 12:32-40 where Jesus spoke about us being ready for His return. Your Bible may have a break between verses 34 and 35. Perhaps it's because of this break that I never noticed the connection between giving to the poor and being ready for Jesus' return.

How does Jesus want to find us when He returns (Luke 12:40)?

Excited   Serving   Sleeping   Ready

Take a look at Luke 12:35 several different translations of this verse.

The idea is clear that when Jesus returns He longs to find His children in the game. The lights are on, because we're not taking a nap from our Christianity or frolicking in the darkness of sin. No! All things have been made new. Jesus has fulfilled the law and given us the grace to live in His power. We're new creatures, and we must evidence the newness He's brought about in our hearts. So get your clothes on, lace up your shoes, and as my friend says to me before watching a big college football game, *get your ankles taped*.

Personal Response: Considering Jesus' return, describe one way you can dress yourself for action, and one way you can keep the lights on?

The truth is we're not going to be generous by accident. Tithing to our churches, giving above and beyond to a ministry, or helping a family member or friend will not magically happen. We have to prepare for it, plan for it, pray over it, and ultimately execute it. Let's bring our good intentions to effective completions. A lost world is waiting. And, who knows, it may be in the middle of our giving that our Master returns and finds us just as He'd always dreamed: ready.

DAY 2
Sowing Generously *(2 Cor. 9:6-15)*

Today we'll finish chapter 9, one of my favorite passages in all of the Bible. I realize I may have too many all-time favorites, and I know what you're thinking: *If you have so many favorites how can each one really be your favorite?* Well, it's like having more than one best friend or more than one favorite pair of jeans. It's possible. And this is what the Bible does to you—spend enough time in it and you'll have a thousand favorites. And each one really will be your favorite. Somehow.

The rest of chapter 9 needs no introduction—except that it's about to be your new favorite. Read 2 Corinthians 9:6-15.

> **We'll discover the remaining six truths about generosity in today's passage. Let's look at numbers 9 and 10. Based on verse 6, circle the correct statement below and fill in #9 on page 112.**

- *The amount you reap has nothing to do with the amount you sow.*

- *The amount you reap is proportionate to the amount you sow.*

- *The amount you reap doesn't matter.*

According to verse 7: *God loves a _____ giver.*

Fill in this phrase as #10 on page 112.

At the time of this writing the steeled soil of winter is about to surrender to spring's lush turf. I'm sharpening my spade. Under winter's reign, my raised beds are but a pile of dead vines and stalks wrapped in each other's arms, dreading the fate that awaits them in the compost pile. I should have tossed them in there months ago, but you know, life happens. At any rate, once the beds are cleaned and spring springs, it will be time to sow. If I tuck my seeds into the ground liberally, I will reap in equal measure. If I do so sparingly, I will harvest in smaller quantity. But something else will also determine my harvest: what I've decided to sow.

Paul mentioned in verse 7 that deciding how much to give is the precursor to actually giving. Every good gardener knows that planting a garden requires decision-making ahead of time. *What will I plant? How much will I plant? Where will I plant?* You don't just start tossing seeds out there without a plan—I did this once and we can talk about how that turned out later. So I want you to consider what decisions God is leading you to make.

1. Do you regularly give to your church?
2. Do you have a surplus over and above your tithe that you can give to a specific need in your church, a ministry, or an individual? How will you determine when and where to give it?
3. What God is asking you to give may not be measured in dollars, but in giving your time or your skills. If any of this resonates with you, decide what the next step should be to obey the Lord.

In the original Greek, Paul used artful alliteration to compose verse 8, with many of the words starting with the letter *p*.

Using the translation in the margin, fill in the following:
God makes all grace abound to the cheerful giver so that
in all _____,
at all _____,
I will have all I_____.

I know few greater joys than giving by faith and watching the Lord provide all I need in ways I couldn't have imagined, fulfilling wants I didn't know I had, blessing me with more than I could have known. This is why this passage is one of my favorites. It has been said that you can't out-give God. It's true, because giving back is His specialty. He blesses us in the most remarkable ways when we give, hardly ever dollar for dollar. Generosity in God's kingdom isn't a Karma based system, praise the Lord! It's way more personal, dynamic, and creative than that. Look back at 2 Corinthians 9:8 and note the ultimate purpose of giving.

You may have been secretly hoping that verse 8 ended with having all you need so you could abound in material wealth. I know the feeling. But when we give generously, God promises to give us everything we need for the good works He intended for us to accomplish. This is by far the greater blessing. You were created to have impact on this earth for God's kingdom. I don't know what works He's called you to, but I know they're good ones that will have eternal results. And I promise, you don't want to miss them for whatever temporal desire you're clinging to. He has something for you to do that will fulfill your heart, mind, and senses more than money or things. And whatever that something is, it's good.

In verse 9, Paul quoted from the Psalms. Read Psalm 112. What is the most meaningful concept to you from this passage?

"And God is able to bless you abundantly, so that in all things at all times, having all that you need, you will abound in every good work."
2 Corinthians 9:8

What strikes me about the generous man in Psalm 112 is his lack of fear. While the psalmist wrote about a generous man, he represents of both genders, so the truth is also applicable for a generous woman. She can freely give, because she's not dependent upon her money to secure her future. She can scatter her gifts to the poor because she doesn't need those gifts to garner friends or prop up her reputation—she trusts God for that. She's not living for the temporary nature of wealth. She is steadfast in the Lord. Money is not her comfort.

So, why is it that having money seems to make us less afraid? In our culture, it seems the most popular word to follow the word *financial* is *security*. We think if we just had the money, all would be well. But that thinking places our hope in something Scripture says will disappear (Prov. 23:5). Money can be a wonderful blessing from God, but it can never take the place of God.

Consider 2 Corinthians 9:10-11. Where does our seed for sowing and bread for eating come from?

In a world of grocery store shelves overflowing with options, it's easy to forget that God is the source of our seed and bread. When I stop and remember that all I have comes from God, it inspires me to give more freely. I trust Him, knowing that all I have is ultimately His, and He has the power to replenish my supply.

Fill in #11 on page 112 with this statement: *God is the ultimate Source of our giving (9:8-10).*

What kind of harvest did God promise us in verse 10?

What is the purpose of being made rich in every way according to verse 11?

In some ways, it seems strange that the reward for the Corinthians' generous giving of their material resources would result in spiritual blessings (harvest of righteousness).

I believe another picture is also at work. Anytime we give generously of our material possessions, the Lord blesses us. Sometimes this comes in the form of financial blessings, but always in the form of spiritual blessings. And don't make the mistake of thinking that the spiritual blessings are less exciting or desirable than the financial ones. The privilege of being part of an eternal harvest of righteousness is one of the greatest joys and adventures of our earthly lives!

DAY 3
Tearing Down Walls *(2 Cor. 10:1-6)*

Today, we begin a new section of 2 Corinthians that will carry us through the end of the letter. You'll remember the first section began with the encouragement of God's comfort (1:1-11). From there Paul clarified why he needed to delay his visit to Corinth while addressing a few other issues in the church (1:12-2:13). Paul went on to explain and defend new covenant ministry, then resumed his travel narrative (2:14-7:16). After praising those who had been faithful in the church, he encouraged them to resume their giving to the poor in Jerusalem (8:1-9:15). Moving forward, we'll mainly see how Paul addressed the stubborn minority trying to take over the church in Corinth. Whether these were false teachers, blatant unbelievers, or those confused in the church, Paul addressed them head on.

You'll notice chapters 10–13 signal a shift in tone. The key is to remember that Paul turned his attention to some specific enemies who were disrupting the church through false teaching.

Part of the disruption in the church included some members specifically attacking Paul for being weak and unimpressive in person. They accused him of putting forth a false image of strength in his letters, while perceiving him to be timid and waffling in person. Paul explained he was anything but weak because of God's divine power at work in his life. He also revealed that the weapons the world uses—and that we're often temped to use—are paltry in comparison to this divine power we have in Christ.

Read 2 Corinthians 10:1-6.

> **Paul reminds us that though we live in the world, we don't _____ like the world does (v. 3).**

Party   Live   War   Behave

> **We use different _____ than the world (v. 4).**

Tools   Weapons   Ingredients   Methods

We know by now that Paul loves a good word picture. Warfare imagery would have been especially familiar to the culture of Paul's day, as Roman soldiers were common in the Mediterranean area. What may not be as obvious to us is that the warfare Paul referenced was a certain type of ancient battle called siege warfare. And siege warfare specifically focused on—you're going to love this—tearing down walls.[3] Anyone need some walls torn down in their lives? In the life of someone you love? Anyone as excited as me about this imagery?

At the top of chapter 10, we find Paul ready to tear down the walls of anti-Christian thinking some outsiders brought to the church at Corinth. Their teachings opposed the gospel and criticized Paul's apostolic authority. This had the potential to create a barrier between Paul and the church, but even worse, to turn the church to rely on a false gospel. Paul wouldn't deal with these false teachers with earthly weapons, because at their core the attacks weren't earthly in nature—they were spiritual onslaughts of false thinking set against God.

Since Paul's critics judged him for being weak, a sufferer, timid, and poor, we can assume some of the weapons they may have expected him to fight with were wealth, prestige, political power, deceit, flatteries, manipulations, and so forth.

Most of us can't relate to being on the frontlines of a battle; however, we've all experienced battles of a different kind. We've come up against the brick walls of jealousy, anger, betrayal, and hurtful friendships. We've scaled a quarter of the way up the rampart of depression, overwhelming emotions, addiction, and paralyzing fear, only to lose our footing and skin ourselves to the bone on the slide back down. We know these battles well. They're the ones that require a full-on siege, but not with the weapons we hold in our hands or find on the self-help aisle.

Since today's text includes several significant words, we're going to look at the original Greek to understand their meanings. The first piece of good news is that we have the power to demolish strongholds. The Greek word is *ochyrōma* and it can mean a castle, stronghold, fortress, fastness, as well as anything on which one relies. In ancient battle, if an opposing army wanted to overtake a city it had to conquer that city's fortress. If the army could demolish the stronghold of the castle, it could capture the whole thing. In verse 5, Paul described what these spiritual strongholds consist of.

The Greek word for the first stronghold we have the power to demolish is *logismos* and it means "thoughts, calculations, reasonings, or reflections."[4] I especially like scholar George H. Guthrie's explanation of these arguments: "walls of wrong thinking that stand in opposition to right Christian teaching."[5]

The word for pretension/high thing is *hypsōma*. It's an elevated structure; in other words, a barrier, rampart, or bulwark. The impression here is a notion contrary to God that's been raised up, lifted high with the purpose to intimidate.

We tend to compartmentalize our wrong thinking and our sin. I simply have discovered the hard way that any thinking that sets itself up against God's Word and His ways will only lead to heartache and pain. We must align our thinking with the Lord's ways, because our behavior follows our thinking.

Now that we know what walls need demolishing (arguments contrary to the Lord along with high, antagonistic pretensions) we need to remember the weapons we have are divine and mighty in power (v. 4). The Greek word for power is *dynatos*.

When it comes to tearing down these seemingly immovable walls, it's so encouraging to know we can pull them down with a power from which the word *dynamite* derived its name. No matter what wall is towering over you, you are not powerless in Jesus.

Look back at the second half of verse 5. In the original language, the phrase *take captive* means to take as prisoner of war.[6] In Paul's case, this meant once he demolished the strongholds of false teaching, he would lead the Corinthians' thinking in the ways of Christ.

Verse 5 might be familiar to you, and you may be thinking, *I've tried that—it doesn't work.* First, ask the Holy Spirit to show you this concept in a fresh way. Second, pay close attention to the order in verse 5. Sometimes we try to take our thoughts captive to Jesus without first dealing with a central sin in our lives. That wall has to come down before we'll have the power to control our thinking.

As we close today's study, reread verse 6. I can't read this verse without thinking of one particularly uncertain season of my life. The Lord and I were doing some serious siege warfare to a few strongholds. I was taking my thoughts captive to Jesus, even if sometimes it felt like trying to keep kittens in a box, as my assistant Bethany likes to say. They jumped out a lot. At one point, I remember wondering when God was going to deal with some of the people who had hurt me. When God was going to focus on them for a while! And then I remember reading those words, when "your obedience is complete." It was as if the Lord was saying to me, *Kelly, just keep doing what I've asked you to do. Keep thinking my thoughts. Keep obeying all the way until you've completed the task. I'll handle everyone else.*

DAY 4
A Soft Answer *(2 Cor. 10:1-2,7-11)*

One of Webster's definitions for the word *practical* is: suitable for everyday use. Despite the cultural differences, ancient practices, and original languages that can differ widely from English, I have never found a book more suitable for everyday use than the Word of God. Today, we'll continue to explore the compassionate yet unbending ways in which Paul addressed those who didn't exactly care for him. You may be in a similar situation in your family or work environment, where you're being unjustly accused or misunderstood. We'll also look at how to respond in those situations. I deliberately skipped over 2 Corinthians 10:1-2 yesterday because it connects well with verses 7-11, which we'll look at in today's study.

First, read 2 Corinthians 10:1 printed in the margin.

Paul was probably being flippant when he said he was "humble" when with them but "bold" when away. His critics must have accused him of these things, a charge Paul kindly but strongly refuted.

With what two characteristics did Paul appeal to the Corinthians?

In our final sessions, we can't forget the gentleness and graciousness of Christ as Paul's foundational tone for the last part of his letter. I'm passionate about these two characteristics because they can positively change our relationships when genuinely implemented. Let's look at them in the Greek. (Note: Your translations may use different English words, which is why we'll use the HCSB version in the margin.)

The original Greek word for *gentleness* describes temperament of mind and heart,[7] while the Greek word behind *graciousness* is more focused on the action of that inward disposition.[8] In other words, if gentleness is the car, then graciousness is how the car drives down the road.

Let's first look at the second word, *graciousness*. The Greek word for *graciousness* here is: *epieikeia*. It means suitableness, equity, mildness—fairness. One scholar, Matthew Arnold, describes *epieikeia* as, "sweet reasonableness."[9] In our world right now, who isn't desperate for some reasonableness? I'd even take it unsweetened. The word can also mean, "making allowances despite facts that might suggest reason for a different reaction."[10] Part of

"Now I, Paul, make a personal appeal to you by the gentleness and graciousness of Christ—I who am humble among you in person but bold toward you when absent." 2 Corinthians 10:1, HCSB

this word, *graciousness*, means we don't have to implement the full use of our power or authority simply because we have it—Paul didn't want to bear down on the Corinthians if he didn't have to.

Let's go back to the first word Paul used to describe the way he appealed to the Corinthians. The Greek word for *gentleness* is *praotēs*, which means "of a soothing disposition."[11] But the word has a deeper meaning that is difficult to translate to English. We tend to think of gentleness as meekness, which can sometimes be perceived as weakness. Rather, gentleness is great power under control. Jesus had the infinite resources of God at His command, yet He surrendered that power by walking in obedience to God. I'll sum it up this way: gentleness is our power fully surrendered to God.

In Galatians 6:1 and in 2 Timothy 2:24-26, this kind, humble, gracious, meek word is specifically directed toward those who are lost, or toward believers who are driving us nuts. I'd like to tell you that when I encounter someone who tests my patience, I just dig deep enough into my heart and eventually hit that stream of gentleness Paul talked about. But look back at verse 1.

Where do gentleness and graciousness come from?

Take a look at 2 Corinthians 10:2 in the NIV. Paul identified his opponents as those who judged him by the world's standards. Some scholars interpret this passage differently, saying that Paul's critics were not evaluating him by the world's standards, but accusing him of living by them—that Paul had acted in some unspiritual way. While these interpretations are not totally unrelated, the emphasis seems to be on evaluation rather than accusation.

We can conclude that the Corinthian dissenters were looking for Paul to be a strong, philosophical orator who could command crowds. They probably expected that a true leader from God would be wealthy and have connections and resources. The troublemakers in Corinth evaluated Paul by the reigning worldly values of the time.

We started with 10:1-2 because they tie into our main reading for today. Read 2 Corinthians 10:7-11.

According to verse 8, what is spiritual authority to be used for? What is it not to be used for?

Paul said his authority was given by the Lord and was to be used for building up the Corinthians. In the same way, our authority is given by God and should be used to build up others. I want this! I want to use whatever God-given authority I have with gentleness and graciousness for the good of others. How much more would the world be drawn to the church if all believers used our spiritual authority, in whatever capacity we have it, for building up other people instead of tearing them down?

This does not mean Paul, or any spiritual leaders for that matter, should be push-overs who never enforce any rules. Here's where the good tension of extending grace and applying discipline comes into play. We need the discernment of the Holy Spirit to know when to emphasize each.

If you struggle with being bossy and bearing down on others, my prayer is that you will learn to display graciousness and gentleness. And if you're continually being walked over and struggle to assert your God-given authority, my prayer is that you'll step up and lead with courage for the sake of building others up—even if that means you have to discipline or correct every once in a while.

DAY 5
Living Your Assignment *(2 Cor. 10:12-18)*

My dad has often described in his sermons the tendency we have as human beings to compare ourselves with one another. Whether we pick up a baseball bat as a young child or try on a dress for the high school prom, we intuitively assess the averages around us. Did I hit the ball further than everyone or not as far as anyone else? Is my dress size bigger or smaller than all the others girls going to the dance? Whether we realize it or not, we perpetually evaluate the average skill sets, appearances, smarts, abilities, and success rates of those around us. We want to know where we fit in this world, and comparing ourselves against one another is one of the ways we try to find out. So, we often default to the law of averages.

Comparing ourselves against a standard isn't all bad. How would we know where to improve or when to be encouraged if we had no mark to reach toward? The trouble and danger come when the standard to which we aspire is based on worldly values, and deem ourselves "successful" when we hit that worldly standard. As you begin today's Scripture reading, my prayer is that the Lord will use this text to free you from measuring sticks that keep you feeling smug or small. Paul offered us a way of measuring ourselves totally different from the world's way. This measure is something that can only come from the Lord. We're in for a great day of study.

Read 2 Corinthians 10:12-18.

Let's revisit our context for a moment. Paul addressed the false apostles and opposing minority who gave him such a hard time. They judged and refuted his ministry by using a measuring rod forged by Corinthian values—wealth, speaking skills, influence, pride, and outward competence, among other things. To win at the comparison game, they had to excel by their own standards and knock down anyone they felt was gaining on them.

Use verse 12 to answer the following:
- **How did Paul describe people who "measure themselves by themselves and compare themselves with themselves"?**

- **What did Paul say he did not do?**

In Paul's context, the problem wasn't comparison thinking per se, but the type of comparison thinking. I see three problems in particular:

1. The opposition set a standard based on worldly values rather than righteousness.

2. The opposition used faulty standards as a way of comparing themselves with one another.

3. The opposition found worth and identity in living up to their man-made standards and found pride in doing it better than everyone else.

Read verse 13 in the margin. The phrase *"area of ministry"* means a portion measured off. The Corinthians were part of God's assignment to Paul, an allotment God had measured off for Paul and his fellow laborers.

Comparison thinking is very dangerous when we do it in spiritual settings. The Enemy loves to sidetrack our ministries by tempting us to evaluate our callings, skill sets, and personalities with those of other believers. And the discouragement we get from comparing ourselves amongst ourselves is easily accessible with the Internet and social media. We can look at other people's activities, social statuses, and vacation excursions with the click of a button. Then, we wonder if what we do, where we go to school, and who our parents are has any meaning. And when we compare ourselves in this way, we will either feel overly proud or like an outright failure.

> "We, however, will not boast beyond measure but according to the measure of the area of ministry that God has assigned to us, which reaches even to you."
> 2 Corinthians 10:13, HCSB

Paul's opponents claimed Corinth as their area of ministry in a blatantly ungodly way. They selfishly bragged about work Paul and his friends labored for, and they taught false doctrine that led believers astray. Though Paul didn't necessarily have the swagger or public speaking chops the false apostles promoted, he had something infinitely grander—an assignment from God. Dear girls, when the Lord entrusts you with a ministry assignment, you will not only *delight* in it, you'll be able to *rest* in it. And if you're pining for someone else's assignment, relinquish that fight. You don't want to encroach on someone else's territory. It will bring you neither joy or satisfaction.

In verse 17 Paul quoted from Jeremiah 9:23-24. Read this passage in the and fill in the blanks.

- **The wise man should not boast in his _____.**
- **The strong man should not boast in his _____.**
- **The wealthy man should not boast in his _____.**

Which of the three are you most likely to be proud about and why?

Jeremiah 9:24 thoroughly reveals who we can boast about and why. Journal the verse in the margin.

Personal Response: Why should we boast about a God who is personal, and who exercises kindness, justice and righteousness on earth?

Turn back to 2 Corinthians 10:18. Who is the one whom God approves?

This is the key we long for: When the Lord entrusts a person, all other earthly comparisons and measuring rods simply don't, well, measure up. Paul could neither measure up to the false apostles' social standing and wealth or worldly influence, nor did he aspire to. He was also unwilling to pat himself on the back in areas where he did excel. The offending Corinthians could play their own game by their own rules with their own made-up goal posts, but Paul wasn't interested in jumping on that team. He was working for a Kingdom not of this world, whose King's approval is the only approval that matters. In John 5:44, Jesus said to the Pharisees, "How can you believe since you accept glory from one another but do not seek the glory that comes from the only God?"

After spending much of my life seeking praise and approval from people, I have never enjoyed a deeper satisfaction than experiencing God's approval and knowing He is pleased. The measuring rods of this world are fundamentally flawed, and they constantly fluctuate. I will continually be selfishly proud or disappointed if the world's standards become the standards by which I measure my worth, or lack thereof. As believers, our lives are about God's glory and loving others, and this frees us from the comparison game.

As we close another week together, I can't tell you how inspired I am by your diligence in getting this far. You've tackled the personal and practical issues of sacrificial giving, tearing down strongholds, threading graciousness and gentleness into your relationships, embracing your God-given assignments, and confronting the pain of comparison thinking. You're so close to finishing 2 Corinthians and gaining a deep understanding of the letter in its entirety! Keep going—the last two weeks of study hold invaluable challenges and encouragement. This is a measuring rod worth reaching for.

THE TIDE
2 Corinthians 11:1–12:10

Topsail Island, North Carolina is a little known treasure. The beaches are pristine, and the sound between the island and mainland boasts a rippling sliver of water that flows both north and south depending on the moon's pull. During the day pleasure crafts zip past the docks, fishermen meander through reeds, and children splash their way out to the sand bars. In the evenings, the sun casts its soft hues over the glinting water. Vacationers scramble to get settled on their decks and docks. No one wants to miss the sunset show.

I vacationed there with a few friends, and one of them suggested we hop in the kayaks and paddle our way across the sound to the mouth of an inlet lined with marshes. Small waterways wind through those marshes—wide enough for a kayak to pass through, long enough for a line to be cast. The fish were calling. Actually they weren't saying anything—they're kind of quiet that way. But we knew they were out there. The swaying reeds, the dive-bombing birds, a telling splash here and there.

We grabbed our rods and oars, a bucket of live shrimp, a crunchy bag of frozen mullet, and off we rowed perpendicular to the choppy current. We lurched in fits and splashes mostly forward because we are not graceful kayakers. After exactly 300 strokes, we made it to the other side and up the bank of a sand bar. We slowly stepped out of our kayaks. Then, we gathered our rods, and April clamored for a shrimp out of the bucket. She pinched him between her fingers and pierced him through with the hook. (At this point in the story, you should know that I don't like to bait my own hook.) For one thing, shrimp are nasty little creatures with beaks (You don't know this if your only exposure to them is at parties dipped in cocktail sauce. And don't even get me started on that black vein).

For an hour and a half I stood knee deep in the ripples, slinging my bait across the inlet's mouth, as if an outdoor magazine was there to do a story on my fishing prowess. Time and again, I tipped the rod back while the shrimp dangled on the hook against the cobalt sky like a popsicle on a stick. *What fish wouldn't want this?* I mused. The perfectly weighted sinker carried the bait across the fluttering waters after I winged the rod forward. The line zinged. The bait dropped beneath the surface of the water. And nothing. Absolutely nothing for 90 minutes other than one truly annoyed sunfish I reeled in. You should also know that I don't like to take my own fish off the hook. But never mind those details. The imaginary outdoor magazine thinks I'm a real talent.

After only attracting one sunfish, we determined to call it a day. We swapped our rods for a net roughly the size of a hammock. We wanted to try to capture a few mud minnows to replenish our supply of live bait before returning home. We are efficient this way. We each grabbed one end of the net and strategically worked our way toward the sand bar. We cornered the mud minnows, and any other unsuspecting creatures like pitifully tiny shrimp and crabs, and with a brisk sweep we scooped them into our clutches. They flapped and scurried around in captivity. This was the most excitement we had all day.

April cupped our winnings in the palms of her hands with the intent of dropping them in the bucket. But when we turned around, the strangest thing had happened. Our boat had vanished. My first thought was: *How in the world had someone stolen our kayak right out from underneath us? We were the only ones ridiculous enough to be out here in the first place!* Then I remembered this little known phenomenon people refer to as the tide. Apparently it had come in, and our kayak had gone out— just like that. Our heads darted in all directions scanning every possible waterway it could have floated down. I panicked. I shot my gaze toward our house, which looked about the size of a Monopoly piece across the waterway. It was way too far to swim. "I see it," April shouted, "I'm going after it!" She yelled back at us while charging waist deep into the current, eventually succumbing to a full swim.

"This is a bad idea," I yelled after her, "We need to call someone to get us!"

That's when April reminded me her phone was in the kayak. *Right.* In the time it took for us to exchange two sentences, we could no longer see the boat. I also spotted a stingray moseying past me, swinging its tail like it had never witnessed a more pathetic situation. I got the feeling that stinging me was beneath him.

April disappeared into the marsh while I waited for rescue. (Because if you're keeping track I don't bait my hooks, unhook my fish, nor do I swim after lost kayaks. I am nothing but baggage, really). After several unnerving minutes the tip of the kayak emerged from the reeds. April was safely inside, rowing toward me. I realized at this point, it would have been well within her rights to leave me out there with my six-ounce sunfish. Instead, she nosed toward me, I climbed in the boat, and we paddled across the sound.

After the kayak debacle, my thoughts drifted to 2 Corinthians. Why? Well, because right now all my thoughts lead there, as if it were Rome. I considered how Paul would plead with the Corinthians to stay in the boat of the gospel, to resist wading out into the tantalizing tide of false teaching that so easily sweeps away one's "sincere and pure devotion to Christ." I thought about cunning and deceptive leaders who presented to the church at Corinth a Jesus who was no Jesus at all. As if in a clashing sea of currents, I heard in my mind Paul bellow from Macedonia for his beloved church to stay afloat in the only gospel that could save them. Abandoning that gospel for something that feels better in the moment or seems more culturally relevant would only leave them stranded in the end.

As I now contemplate this section of Paul's letter, I'm reminded that the times haven't changed all that much. The tides that clamor for our beliefs and affections never cease being on the move. They continue to creep up on us almost undetectably, until the day we turn our heads while out of the boat, and everything we thought we knew is gone. But it doesn't have to be this way. As we begin Session 6, my prayer is that the Holy Spirit will help us tighten up our theology where it's gotten sloppy. If you've cracked your heart open to someone or something that is leading you astray, I urge you to run back to the Scriptures. We'll be reassured by the steadfast truths of the Word, reminded that whatever the world promises us may flow in today, but it will flow out tomorrow. Only the Jesus Paul preached will prove unsinkable enough to hold us.

Group Guide (Week 6)

Prepare

Review your notes and answers from Session 5, and ask God to prepare your heart for the group time. Try to get in touch with someone else in the group who you haven't seen lately to encourage them to come back.

Review & Discuss

Flip through your homework from Session 5 and review each day, noting anything important that you might want to share. If you missed any of the following during the homework for Sessions 4 and 5, look the answers up now and list them here.

Eleven Truths About Generosity

See pp. 81-82:

1.

2.

See p. 85:

3.

4.

5.

See p. 88:

6.

7.

See pp. 96-97:

8.

9.

10.

See p. 99:

11.

Review these truths about generosity and discuss how these should shape and change our thinking about giving. Consider the following questions as well.

After studying what a lifestyle of generosity looks like, what is most difficult about giving for you?

Considering the homework from Day 3, what walls in your heart need to be torn down—walls you're powerless to handle yourself?

Is wrong thinking attached to these walls? How have worldly weapons failed you? Consider all the things you've tried that rely on self or worldly wisdom.

So many of our problems and struggles can be traced back to our thinking. Consider these familiar expressions: "It's in your head," "don't overthink it," and "the power of positive thinking." Because we know so much of the battle is in our minds, we think if we could just control our thoughts, then we could get a handle on things. We also know this is much more difficult than it sounds. And sometimes, it's because we're making it difficult! We do this when we believe and embrace thoughts that are contrary to God's Word.

Review Day 4, which begins on page 103. Then consider the following questions.

How do you see a sense of worldly evaluation of Christian leaders in today's Christian culture? For example, do we judge our pastors or spiritual leaders based on appearance, size of church, social media followers? How might these "worldly standards" negatively affect our churches?

In what specific relationship in your life could you stand to be more gracious, measured, mild, reasonable? Explain.

Journal
What recurring negative thoughts do you battle and keep coming back to, even after having experienced real victory in a certain area? List two thoughts below, and next to each one, write what it would look like to make them obedient to Christ.
- Stray, defeating thought #1:

- Stray, defeating thought #2:

Take Action
Think through some practical ways you can show generosity to others this week. Are there unbelievers you know who you can be praying for and pointing to Christ? Take some time to pray for them now.

- **Memorize:** 2 Corinthians 12:9
  Use a note card or write this verse on a mirror or somewhere where you will see it often. This should be a reminder of how God's grace is all we need and how His power is made perfect in our weaknesses.

DAY 1
Pure Jealousy *(2 Cor. 11:1-6)*

I generally try to present myself as a relaxed and cheery person. Especially when I'm stressed—maybe it's an overcompensation of sorts. Try as I might, people still think I'm intense. *Me, intense?* I think. And though they kindly play along, my friends never act surprised by this assumption. No matter how breezy I try to be, the intensity is still visible to the people around me.

I don't know if Paul would have described himself as passionate, intense, or given to stress. Maybe he fought his intensity, as I occasionally do. No one ever called Paul laid-back. In this session's study, we'll see how Paul's passion and zeal reached new heights out of love for the Corinthians and the true gospel he preached. I'm thinking Paul could have benefited from the calming enzymes of certain super foods to deal with certain super apostles, but I don't know if he had access to that kind of food in Corinth. Plus, I'm thinking that if there ever was something to be fired up about, it's people's souls! It's the gospel. It's Jesus Christ! So let's dig in. I have no doubt we will see our own cultures and communities represented in chapter 11, and become more aware of the things that truly deserve our passion.

Read 2 Corinthians 11:1-6.

> **What word does Paul use to describe his feelings for the Corinthians in verse 2?**

> **Look back at Exodus 20:1-5. What similarity do you see between God's passion for the Israelites and Paul's passion for the Corinthians?**

Here's a definition for jealousy:
> "A strong feeling of possessiveness, often caused by the possibility that something which belongs, or ought to belong, to one is about to be taken away."[1]

We often think negatively of jealousy. I hate the feeling of being captive to jealousy's consuming nature—it often leads to reckless and harmful actions. But there's a difference between being jealous *of* someone and being jealous *for* someone. And there's a difference between jealousy that finds its source in our flesh versus the Spirit.

Why was Paul jealous for the Corinthians? How did he describe his jealousy?

I wouldn't want to serve a passive God any more than I would want to be best friends with someone who didn't care what happened in my life. In the purest sense of the word, we cannot be jealous for another person if we don't first care for that person. Paul deeply cherished the Corinthians, which is why he was jealous for them. It sounds strange to write, but I want to be more jealous. Jealous for the lost. Jealous for my friends, family, and the people I minister to, to know Jesus more deeply. We simply won't have the energy for godly jealousy if we don't care about another person's spiritual condition.

Verse 4 is the key to understanding the heart of the problem in the church of Corinth. What three distortions did Paul point out?

I want to consider the progression here. First of all, the battle starts with the mind. Just as the serpent in the garden challenged Eve's thinking, so the false teachers in Corinth went after the believers' minds. They challenged their Christ-centered thinking, beliefs, and worldviews. And they did so convincingly, wooing the Corinthians away from the true Jesus, His Spirit, and the pure gospel.

Paul warned that just as the Serpent deceived Eve, we too can be deceived. But if being deceived means to be tricked or misled, how can we know when it's happening to us? Reading and studying God's Word and letting it dwell in us will always be one of the chief ways we can protect our minds from the deceptions of the Enemy. If we toy with or buy into a way of thinking that is contrary to God's Word, we're on the road to deception. If what we begin to believe doesn't match up with God's Word we can know we're being deceived. So in a sense, we don't know when we're being deceived unless we let the Word of God tell us.

Look back at verse 4. What was the result of the preaching of a false Jesus?

When someone preaches a false Jesus, and we open ourselves to a counterfeit gospel, we tread on dangerous ground. At the end of verse 4, Paul said that the Corinthians had no problem with the critics teaching a different Jesus! They received it without being troubled in any way. You, too, may be struggling with a once tightly held biblical belief: You are no longer sure it's true because of what you've recently read, watched, or experienced. Go back to the Word, and find the truth.

When the Enemy comes to deceive us, he does so cunningly. Remember, the serpent in the garden of Eden was cursed to crawl on his belly after Eve ate of the tree. There's no telling how charming he may have looked, or with what swagger he strutted into the garden before twisting God's Word. He must have seemed believable, his arguments buyable, his promises desirable for Eve to have been deceived. This is why we must continually immerse ourselves in the Word. When the tantalizing winds of culture's "liberating arguments" blow through our thoughts, we can then protect ourselves from being lulled into devastating deception by countering false wisdom with biblical truth.

Paul couldn't bear to see the false teachers in Corinth lead his new converts astray. But notice, he didn't fear the Corinthians being led astray from religion, a denomination, or even from his own self. He was afraid they'd be led away from their pure devotion to Christ! This is why Paul's jealousy fell in the *godly* category. His sole passion was to deliver the Corinthians to Jesus, pure, as a father would present his daughter as a bride to her bridegroom. As we start Session 6, I'm jealous for you to know the difference between the world's cunning teaching and the wisdom of Jesus. I'm jealous for you to see the thinness of materialism against the adventure of a Christ-following life. I'm jealous for you to know the satisfying love of Jesus, sold out for no other. This is pure jealousy.

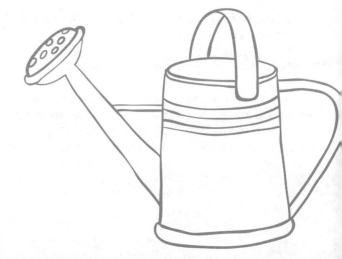

DAY 2
What Matters Most *(2 Cor. 11:5-15)*

Our culture places a premium on beauty, talent, skill level, wealth, social status, charisma, people skills, and fame. Paul's Corinth was no different. Even in the church today, we gravitate to those we deem successful, rather than those we deem common. We've probably all thought how awesome it would be for a specific movie star or famous athlete to become a Christian. But we may not have that same thought about the widow at the end of our street or the troubled middle class family in our neighborhood. This is not to say that being a professional athlete or movie star is inherently sinful or shouldn't be pursued with the right heart. The problem comes when outward appearance and social standing are what we use to evaluate spiritual worth or success—our own or someone else's.

The church at Corinth had stumbled into that very trap, buying into the teachings and claims of the false apostles simply because these men were persuasive, charismatic, and influential. Paul had quite an impressive list of accomplishments to his name as well, but either the Corinthians didn't value those achievements, or Paul chose to withhold some of them so as not to take away from the pure power of the gospel.

Read 2 Corinthians 11:5-15.

> **According to the Corinthians, what skill(s) did it seem Paul lacked (v. 6)?**

> **List all the ways Paul humbled himself so he wouldn't be a burden to the Corinthians.**

Paul couldn't win with the Corinthians. If he charged them a fortune to minister in their church, then they would have called him a charlatan; when he didn't charge them at all, they were offended. Most speakers in ancient Corinth were paid professionals, and those who came to listen expected to pay, hoping part of their money could purchase them closeness to the speaker. If Paul had allowed the Corinthians to support him financially, then they may have tried to use it as leverage to control him or his message. Also, Paul's manual labor as a tentmaker was an embarrassment to them; as one scholar said, "an impoverished leader was a contradiction in terms."[2] Even though Paul brought the life-changing message of Jesus, it didn't come in the manner the Corinthians wanted. Now, we're getting an idea of how political ministry had become in

Corinth. Still, Paul refused to change from a humble approach to a conceited one. Oddly enough, his humble service was something he actually boasted about.

Review verse 11. What reason did Paul give for choosing to humbly serve the Corinthians?

The Corinthians would have been happier with Paul if he had served and loved them according to their specific ideas and conditions. They wanted Paul relying on their pay so he could be subject to them. They demanded that he fit into their social norms by dropping the lowly tent-making gig and jumping on the speaking circuit. The problem was that their plans would have undermined Paul's pure love for them. To minister under the constructs of the Corinthian culture was really no ministry at all.

To get a better picture of the flashy Corinthian approach versus Paul's humble service, read 1 Corinthians 2:1-5. List all the ways Paul ministered and the ways he didn't.

The Ways Paul Ministered	The Ways Paul Didn't Minister

Continue reading 1 Corinthians 2:5-7,10.

What word was used several times to characterize Paul's message?

Intellect   Charm   Charisma   Wisdom

How do we get this (v. 10)?

Paul wasn't saying we shouldn't work hard at our crafts or refine our skills and talents. He also was not promoting laziness, or leaning on the convenient excuse that the Spirit will somehow take care of our unpreparedness. (I've tried to fall back on this one a time or two.) In context, the Corinthian false teachers attempted to dissuade people from the true gospel by their sharp speaking skills and intelligence. Paul pointed out that human pride and smarts are no match for God's wisdom and power. Whether we are skilled or unskilled, educated or uneducated, the power of the gospel shines through humble vessels.

As I write this, I'm in the midst of preparing to lead worship at an event for ministry leaders. I could list countless people who have broader singing ranges and silkier voices with guitar skills that pick circles around my strumming. I'm working hard, but I'm limited in my abilities. When I look at a passage like this, I'm encouraged, even in my shortcomings, because I can pray and trust that the power of God will rest upon me as I lead worship.

Turn back to 2 Corinthians 11:6. Instead of being a trained speaker, what did Paul say he had?

Don't miss this, girls. We live in a world where people don't know where they're going. They don't know what to hope in or if hope even exists. Many don't know why they're here. They're chasing every imaginable dream, only to realize it wasn't what they wanted. For a season maybe they woke up for a certain pleasure, but one day that pleasure stopped satisfying or walked out the door. But you and I don't live with that emptiness. We have the knowledge and wisdom Paul wrote about because God has revealed it to us by His Spirit (1 Cor. 2:10)! And the knowledge He revealed is "the knowledge of God's glory displayed in the face of Christ" (2 Cor. 4:6). And we carry this treasure in jars of clay, not refined, showy vessels (2 Cor. 4:7)!

The wisdom and knowledge of Jesus is what the world is desperate for. We don't have to be experts in the latest trends, or have razor sharp skills designed to make people covet our positions, buy others' respect, or impress them with our beauty. The world has all this in spades! What people need is for those of us with spiritual wisdom and knowledge to tell them about what truly matters. They need someone to tell them the secret wisdom of God that rescues us from loneliness, gratifies our longings, obliterates the strongholds that keep us addicted, and washes our consciences clean!

Plain and simple, this secret wisdom is cultivated by time in God's Word. It's quickened in prayer. It's deepened by fellowship with other believers. It's revealed in greater degrees when we're obedient. You can't buy the secret things of God, but He's pleased to give them to the ones who seek Him.

DAY 3
A Foolish Boast *(2 Cor. 11:16-30)*

Today's passage is an interesting one to say the least. It's not often we hear the apostle Paul say he did not speak as the Lord would or according to His ways. That didn't mean Paul was no longer under God's authority—it means he took his Christianity off-roading into the woods after the Corinthians, because he tried everything else to convince them of his apostleship. If he couldn't beat his opponents, he would momentarily join them in their tactics, but not for their goals—that's the key difference. Paul stooped to the bragging shenanigans of the false teachers, but only to ultimately prove his undying love and commitment to the church at Corinth and to turn their sights back to Jesus. If you ever thought Christianity was simply a matter of following a list of rules, today will prove it's far more relational and creative than that. Not to mention adventurous.

Read 2 Corinthians 11:16-30.

Paul's situation sounds similar to ours today: charming, charismatic personalities who claim to love God, and may even claim to follow Jesus, yet are leading countless believers down paths that are at odds with God's Word. The Corinthian church was filled with new believers who were especially vulnerable to the pull of the super apostles. These false teachers claimed to be God's leaders but were actually about their own position and power. Paul had no choice but to go head-to-head with them for the sake of the church he loved.

> **According to verse 30, what did Paul boast about? Why do you think he boasted about these things?**

The Lord has used today's passage to convict me. Honestly, I like to stay out of the fray. I'm not one to jump into controversy. I fear people twisting my words, I hate being misunderstood, and I generally dislike being disliked. (Did you notice my fears are all about me?) Pretty much all the controversy that swirls around taking a stand is everything I try to avoid. In other words, no one has to worry about me running for president. We are in a battle, though, and the Lord has not called us to live our lives slinking away from uncomfortable situations. If the world is going to use its megaphone to sway the people to whom we're called to be ministers of reconciliation, then how much more should you and I boast about who Jesus is and what He has done in our lives?

Personal Reflection: Consider the way people who are not believers (or confused believers) flaunt and promote their false beliefs. How do you counter that by boasting about Jesus and what He has done in your life? If this is hard for you, list what stands in your way.

Review verse 20. Keep in mind Paul was not referring to a hypothetical situation, but a real one that affected the church in Corinth. List the five harmful actions the church put up with from the false teachers.

When I read this list I think, why in the world would anyone put up with this? But I don't have to look too far, either around me or into my own history, to see we all tolerate misconduct from others we should never allow. Remember, these enemies masqueraded as apostles of Christ and servants of righteousness—they didn't obviously look evil (2 Cor. 11:13-15). I tend to forget this! I think of them as evident evildoers in scary black hats. Get that out of your head. They spoke with Jesus-like persuasion.

I personally experienced this at an impressionable time in my life. I desperately wanted to be on the inside of some dynamic personalities who were "spiritual" but not Christ-like. I put up with all kinds of nonsense, never knowing when I was going to be chosen or left out. I allowed them to lie to and take advantage of me. After awhile I even let myself become deceived, all because I wanted acceptance. Praise God, a few people like Paul stepped into my life. They reminded me of what healthy, godly friendships look like in comparison to the misery I experienced.

"You even put up with anyone who...
1.

2.

3.

4.

5.   "

Paul essentially said he was too weak for the kind of harsh treatment the false leaders displayed (v. 21). How was Paul's approach to ministry with the Corinthians different than the false teachers? What Christ-like characteristics did Paul display?

If you're wondering if someone is a true servant of the Lord, ask yourself these questions: Is the person humble or proud? Gentle or harsh? Patient or explosive? A bragger of self-made accomplishments or a boaster of weaknesses that makes much of Jesus' strength?

Paul's words in verses 22-29 are what many refer to as "The Fool's Speech." As my friend Julie put it, "Paul didn't mention his humble service earlier, he was just doing it, and they forced him to come out and say what before he was just trying to show with his choices, his life, his work, his words."

What descriptions of identity and heritage did Paul begin with in verse 22? Why start here with his boasting?

Why do you think Paul said he had lost his mind to talk like this (v. 23)?

Review verses 24-27.

What were some of the physical difficulties Paul endured in ministry?

Have you faced anything of the kind in order to share the gospel? Would you be willing to? Explain.

I've included verses 28-29 for you here: "Besides everything else, I face daily the pressure of my concern for all the churches. Who is weak, and I do not feel weak? Who is led into sin, and I do not inwardly burn?"

When I look at the whole of this speech I'm challenged. Paul leveraged his heritage, experiences, trials, and an open heart to defend himself before the church he served. The persuasive personalities who looked like Christ's ministers, and who were holding power over the Corinthian believers, needed someone to stand up to them. We need people willing to take a stand for truth today. We're desperate for people to rise up with humility, for the sake of others, so Jesus can receive glory. If we fling ourselves out there with any other motives—even if we speak truth—we will be as foolish as the ancient false teachers.

If you consider yourself too weak or powerless to make any kind of difference, read Revelation 12:10-11 as an encouraging reminder.

Your testimony, along with the power of the blood of the Lamb, has the ability to do what?

Personal Response: Don't rush to finish today. Take a moment to prayerfully journal about one specific way you can step up and take a necessary stand. I'm praying for the strength to do the same.

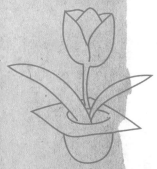

DAY 4
Caught Up To Heaven *(2 Cor. 11:30-33; 12:1-6)*

First off, let me begin by saying I'm so proud of you! Not many people get this far into a Bible study. The chores of life creep in, enthusiasm wanes, and friends drop out. Then you're left with that awkward task of going to your group meeting alone, when all you really want is to be home on your couch with a bowl of cheese dip. I understand this. I want you to know that the cheese dip will come and go, but your time in the Word of God will never be taken from you. When Mary of Bethany sat at Jesus' feet as Martha served the meal, Jesus said that Mary's investment of time with Him would never be taken from her (Luke 10:42). Be encouraged. This is time well spent that will echo into eternity.

As I commend you on your discipline and commitment, according to today's text I should be cheering you on for your weaknesses as well. Once again, Paul showed us that we can take great joy in our frailties—not for frailties' sake, but because the power of Christ shines magnificently through our weakness.

Read 2 Corinthians 11:30-33.

Were you perplexed by Paul inserting his account of being lowered in a basket from a window in the wall of Damascus? At first this struck me as an odd story in an odd place. I tucked it away as "The Great Basket Mystery." (I have a large folder in my head for similar Bible questions.) Thankfully, there is additional information in Acts that sheds further light. Before reading the text, keep in mind Paul's prestigious heritage and upbringing as a Jew of Jews. Also note that the great basket escape happened soon after his salvation experience on the road to Damascus.

Read Acts 9:20-25.

Paul had gone from being renowned in the Jewish community as a Pharisee intent on stomping out this movement called the Way (Acts 9:1-2), to a man on the run as a follower of it's founder, Jesus. Explain how going from being a powerful leader to a fugitive fleeing for his life would be considered a weakness Paul could boast about.

We can all take a page out of Paul's evangelism and discipleship playbook here. Sharing what God has done in our friendships, schools, families, and so on—especially during times of weakness and vulnerability—is one of the most genuine ways to share our faith.

A friend of mine shared this story with me: "I remember a man coming in to service the cable. He said, 'Lady, is your house always this clean?' I told him, 'I used to be a real pig!' What happened to change you?' he asked. 'The Lord Jesus Christ,' I replied. I never expected to share about Jesus that day in that way. It is always exhilarating! I have grown to absolutely love the simple and unglamorous ways God can use us. It speaks more of His greatness to me that He cares about such little details."

Turn back to 2 Corinthians and read verses 12:1-6. What heaven was Paul caught up to?

First	Second
Third	Fourth

According to verse 4, what types of things did Paul hear?

Why did Paul speak about himself in the third person? Some scholars suggest he didn't want to come off as arrogant about this extraordinary experience, so he used this grammatical tool to humbly detract attention from himself. Sharing about the amazing works God has done in our lives is vital for us to do, but we should be careful not to slip into a "bragimony." (One of my favorite made up Christian terms for when a testimony turns into bragging about how awesome we are.)

When sharing about God's goodness in your life, what's one specific thing you can do to make sure God is the One being celebrated instead of exalting yourself?

While many theories abound concerning "the third heaven," many scholars say Paul referred to the highest heavenly realm, God's throne room, paradise. "It may be, therefore, that Paul was taken into the very presence of God in the heavenly holy of holies."[3] Paul's experience fits well with the obsession our modern culture—even secular culture—has with the afterlife and spirituality. Granted, much of what we watch on television or in movies about the spiritual realm is skewed or completely false. However, this fascination with spirituality tells me that we inherently know we're more than physical beings who exist only for this fading earth.

Why do you think Paul felt the need to share this experience with the Corinthians after keeping it private for 14 years?

Paul wasn't sure if his heavenly experience took place in the body or out of the body. Either way, Paul was comfortable with how the Lord chose to snatch him up. What I find meaningful is that both times Paul claimed to not know the answer to this mystery, he insisted, God knew.

Look back at the end of verse 6. What two things did Paul want to be noted for?

This is one of those enormously practical verses skimmed over my whole life, until now. After Paul relayed one of the most sacred, holy, extraordinary experiences a person could ever have, he essentially said, "But enough about all that. The real reason I want you to trust my apostleship is because of the way I've lived my life before you. By what I do and say." We love the sensational. We get excited for a miracle, or a good vision or dream. We're infatuated with celebrities, those with a big name or a big ministry (for bigness' sake), maybe even more so today. But do we have the same level of passion for daily faithfulness? The humble service no one sees? The patient and kind word spoken in mundane conversations? Supernatural and extra-special experiences are wonderful, but it's the consistent godly patterns of our lives that yield enduring fruit.

The Lord snatching a person up for anything—especially a visit to heaven—is an unspeakable privilege and blessing. I've had a few experiences in my life I would categorize as extraordinarily sacred or holy. At times, the Lord has spoken to my heart more clearly than if I'd heard Him audibly. He's given me experiences I would say were divine. I treasure these, and occasionally I share about them. You may have some, too. But at the end of our lives, these mountain top experiences will not be what we're remembered for. By God's grace, we will make a difference for Christ by what we've said and done. Because of how we've humbly, sacrificially, and all-out joyfully lived our lives with day-to-day faithfulness, we will be remembered.

Our culture makes much of the spotlight and the sensational. We even fall into this trap in the church sometimes. The bright lights will fade, and the stage will one day have someone else dance across its surface. But those who do the will of the Lord will live forever (1 John 2:17). And His will is to love Him and love others. Let's do this in word and deed.

DAY 5
When I'm Weak, I'm Strong *(2 Cor. 12:7-10)*

When I'm weak, I am strong
Suffering brings Your grace along
My deepest hurt becomes my greatest song
For when I'm weak I am strong

I wrote these words and put them to a simple melody when I was in college. It was my little chorus I strummed on my guitar, sometimes singing through tears. I was always a pretty serious kid—that one of my favorite passages of Scripture growing up was about Paul's thorn in the flesh and that I wrote a chorus about it, is a testament to this. This is still one of the most meaningful passages in the Bible to me. Not so much because I identify with the thorn, but because of the presence of Jesus who presses in deeper than the thorn. I'm praying you'll be encouraged by today's reading.

Read 2 Corinthians 12:7-10.

The Greek word for thorn is *skolops* and can refer to "something sharp or pointed, such as a splinter or a stake."[4] Paul used this metaphor to speak of a particular pain that was difficult and unceasing. He also told us the thorn was inherently evil, calling it "a messenger of Satan" (v. 7). Let's look at the why, what, and who of the thorn.

Why The Thorn Was Given
Why was the thorn given (v. 7)?

Personal Response: Why would Paul becoming proud or conceited be one of the worst things that could happen to him, his ministry, and his relationship with the Lord?

Of the why, what, and who of Paul's thorn in the flesh, the why is most clearly answered. As a result of Paul's supernatural experience with the Lord, he would need this thorn to keep him walking in humility. We may not have all the information we'd like, but let's give it up for at least one clear answer!

What The Thorn Was
Several ideas and opinions have been offered as to the nature of Paul's thorn, but the reality is we simply don't know. Some believe it was a physical ailment, others believe it was persecution and opposition, still a few think it was psychological travail. You can

make arguments for any of these; however, a physical condition and persecution of some sort are the two with the most traction.

In one way, I'd love to know what Paul's thorn in the flesh was. Reading his letters with that knowledge in mind would give us more insight into his writings. At the same time, I'm glad we don't know. That makes this passage more broadly applicable to any of us who have a "thorn." We don't need to have *Paul's* thorn to experience the grace and power of Jesus; we only need to have *a* thorn. Lacking the thorn's specific identity, we focus on Jesus during our suffering rather than comparing our thorn to the nature of Paul's. If our thorn matched Paul's, consider how that one form of suffering might be exalted. I think the Lord saved us big by not revealing this one.

The Who Behind The Thorn
The difficulty of this verse is that it's not crystal clear who the giver was—God or Satan. However, we do know "this word was usually employed to denote that God's favor had been bestowed."[5] We also know that God chose to not remove it and that He had a good purpose for the thorn. My personal belief, and the view of scholars I've studied, is that God was the giver of the thorn. I know this can be difficult to accept—it's hard for me to accept—especially since we know the thorn was evil. Regardless of whether you view God or Satan as the giver, tension exists. Either God gave the thorn, which has its obvious difficulties, or Satan gave it while God stood by and allowed it.

Personal Reflection: What challenges you the most in understanding God's character in either giving the thorn Himself, or allowing Satan to give the thorn in verse 7?

We're not the first people to struggle with this question: If God is good, how could He give an evil thorn or permit pain He could have stopped? We also see this play out in John 11. Mary and Martha's brother Lazarus was deathly ill. They sent for Jesus while their brother was still alive, pleading for Jesus to come and heal him. But Jesus didn't come in time (11:17).

Read John 11:33-37.

Mary and Martha's Jewish friends had two very different responses when they saw Jesus weep alongside Mary. What were they? What was the chief complaint about Jesus from the second group?

The other day, I took one of those walks with the Lord where I prayed, praised, and also contended. I confessed to the Lord that one of the greatest challenges to my faith is seeing the lost dying without the gospel. But also, it's very difficult for me to watch tragedies fall on believers and unbelievers alike that God has the power to stop. If He knew the trajectory of this decaying world and our wicked hearts, why start this whole thing in the first place? I was hashing these questions out with the Lord on my walk—not expecting an answer, but more interested in receiving a deeper assurance of His great love for the world.

A few hours later, I was thumbing through the passage you just read. I've read John 11 bunches of times, but had never noticed the significance of the two distinct responses to the exact same event. Both groups witnessed Jesus weeping with Mary near Lazarus' tomb. One group's eyes were opened to Jesus' profound love for Lazarus—"See how He loved him" (v. 36). But the other group was filled with a sea of doubt—"If He has the power to heal, why didn't He?" The first group was focused on what Jesus had done; the second on what He could have done but didn't. Now, flip back to 2 Corinthians to see Paul's response to Jesus.

After Paul heard from Jesus, his tone significantly changed. He went from pleading with the Lord to remove the thorn to what entirely new response?

The thorn had not changed, but Paul's perspective had. Instead of solely seeing the evil of the thorn and focusing on the pain of it, he realized it was an avenue through which Christ's power could rest upon him. The great pain was accompanied by an even greater joy!

I pray that you're encouraged today by this difficult passage. If we weren't given verses 9-10, we might find ourselves despairing over verses 7-8. Rather, if we choose to seek the Lord's response to our difficulties, whether a persistent thorn or other hardships, we will experience the miracle of being glad in sadness, boasting about weakness, and delighting in suffering.

A dear friend of my family's recently went through one of the most devastating losses a person can endure. He tweeted this: "God, you permit what you could have prevented. Thank you. My heart trusts in your unfailing love." This is the miracle I'm talking about. A heart of thanks and trust in the Lord who may give or allow the thorn, but never does so without also giving the grace and power of Jesus in extra measure. For when we're weak, we're strong.

ALL THINGS NEW

2 Corinthians 12:11–13:14

As we begin our final session together, I pray our theme verse will anchor you for the rest of your days: "Therefore, if anyone is in Christ, he is a new creation; old things have passed away, and look, new things have come." (2 Cor. 5:17, HCSB). Who doesn't love the concept of being made new in Christ? Swelling with hope is the image of the old emptying out to sea as the new sweeps in like rolling waves charging toward the shore. Writing about this reality has further defined my hope as a believer and my expectation for change.

The troubling catch is that, as much as the idea lures me in, it also leaves me frustrated. What I mean is, I love the reality of being a new person in Christ, but I'm still here with a decent helping of what feels obviously old. My family and friends will vouch for me. Sure, I can without a doubt see more Christ-likeness defining my life, but still—the old doesn't feel like it's passed away quite like I'd hoped; the new doesn't feel as though it's come quite as decisively as the verse reads.

Let me clarify a bit. Yesterday, I was inexcusably irritable with a friend who was helping me with a computer problem. While she hung over my shoulder I could hear her chewing—didn't she realize this was no time for mouth sounds? I've been swatting at critical thoughts toward others, more so than normal, like flies buzzing around in my brain that somehow keep slipping into my thinking. Why can't my thoughts eagerly default to the good work that God is doing in people instead of locking onto what bothers me or where they're falling short? I went to bed last night feeling more not-married than usual, wondering why my life looks so far outside the bell curve. I could list a few other things, but you know old when you see it. It's so awfully familiar.

Maybe you can relate. Maybe that same familiar habit is back in your life and brought along its perpetually self-centered cousins, discontentment and negativity. You wonder how Paul could say with surety and confidence that the old has gone and the new has come, especially when the old seems so present, and the new seems to have gotten lost on the way.

So what does a verse like this mean?

Remember, the context in which Paul wrote was overflowing with people who judged one another by human standards. It was all about how well you performed, what you could achieve, and how good you looked while pulling off the whole shebang—you've studied this thoroughly. (The culture was hardly preaching dependence on Jesus.) Paul refuted this man-centered way of thinking by explaining that something revolutionary had happened: "The old has gone, the new has come!" The new covenant has replaced the old one. We now live by the Spirit and Jesus dwells within us. And all of creation is under a new order.

So we don't need to be defined by how well we do based on a behavioral point system, and we don't have to find our worth in our achievements. Rather, a sweeping change happened in the universe when Jesus made us righteous through His death and resurrection. (This is not to mention the formation of a thriving new community called the church or creation itself having been freed from the old regime of death, one day to be entirely redeemed.)

In this context, Paul painted the grand scene of redemption with the bold and decisive brushstrokes of "old" and "new." This is big picture stuff. "Therefore, if anyone is in Christ, he is a new creation" (2 Cor. 5:17, HCSB). Things just became really personal—"if anyone is in Christ." When we're in Christ, He starts rewriting the script of our lives. We're no longer starring in the old play of our selfish desires and lusts. The whole plot changes, because we're not content to live for ourselves anymore but for the One who died and was raised for us (2 Cor. 5:15). We now see everyone around us with new eyes because of who each one is in Christ or who each one can be in Him.

Still you ask, why then am I battling the old stuff when I've been made new? I wonder if the answer isn't tucked away a few verses later in 2 Corinthians 6:1, where Paul urged us not to receive God's grace in vain. Even as a new person in Christ, I can choose to live by the old script. I can nurture my pride and slip in a few morsels of gossip at the table and indulge at the troughs of temptation. I can choose the world's company as my closest community. I can cultivate unforgiveness, because it feels safer than the alternative. I'm free to wound those who have hurt me or withhold good from those who need me. In other words, I believe it's possible to be new with old clothes on, though this is positively a miserable way to exist.

Personally, I have struggled with things like a critical spirit, selfishness, and pettiness, to name a few. But when I remember that I am in Christ as a new creation—which are states of being, not my current performance level—I'm propelled to fall into step with the newness Christ has brought about in my life. Moment by moment, I can choose to comply with the new—to receive God's grace for its intended purpose. It requires some fortitude and starving our selfishness, but there's nothing like growing into the woman Jesus has made you to be. Absolutely nothing like it. And do not for one second believe Satan's lie that you just happen to be the one person on earth for whom Jesus only made a little bit new. Own your new creation-ness.

In day to day terms, this means we can put other people's desires ahead of our own, we can correct the course of our thinking by being in the Word and having our minds renewed, and we will seek the humble heart of Christ instead of our arrogance and pride. We'll rely on the God-sized power we have to tear down the bars of thinking and behavior that keep us stuck. When we feel unattractive and unchosen, we can fall into our Comforter who draws near to us, assuring us we're not alone. When we don't know how to chart our path, He gives wisdom. When we're impatient or critical, we confess and don't have to wonder if we'll be forgiven—restoration is in full supply. When we're attacked, we have an arsenal of surprisingly powerful spiritual weapons at our disposal.

Yes, everything is different now. Everything is new. All we need to do is receive God's grace so we can live as though it's true.

Group Guide (Week 7)

Prepare
Recall some of what you have learned from Paul's letter to the church at Corinth. Then pray for the other girls in your group by name, specifically that the truths from 2 Corinthians would sink into their hearts and help them grow in their relationship with Christ.

Review & Discuss
Look back through the Session 6 homework, and circle or highlight anything you want to focus in on during the following time with your group. Consider the discussion questions that follow, and jot down any questions you had regarding the homework and what you're studying in 2 Corinthians.

The following is a personal relationship evaluation. Read and think through the questions on your own first, then come together with your group to share.

If you're trying to decipher if the jealousy you're experiencing is godly or from your flesh, consider these questions:
- *Is your ultimate goal for the person to love Jesus with an undivided heart, or to be attached to you?*
- *Are you trying to control this person for your own purposes or liberate him or her?*
- *Are you consumed by what you want this person to do for you, or how desperately you want them in relationship with Christ?*

In what ways do you find your biblical worldview being opposed? It may be through personal opposition or it could be more general, such as through the media, books, Hollywood. How is the opposition cunning or compelling? Be honest in your reflection.

Think of a time when you received a compromised version of Christ or His gospel as truth. What caused you to be deceived?

Read Galatians 5:6-12 aloud as a group if you have the time to see what Paul said to the Christians in Galatia as they faced false doctrine making its way into their churches.

Review your homework from Day 3 and Day 4 of Session 6, then answer the following questions.

Read 2 Corinthians 11:30. Then consider this question: Given the circumstances he faced with the Corinthian church, why would Paul choose to boast about his weaknesses instead of his strengths?

Can you think of an especially weak time in your life when Jesus showed Himself strong? Describe some ways you can share this experience with believers and unbelievers alike that makes the hope of Jesus accessible and relatable.

Review Day 5 of your homework from Session 6, and then consider the following questions:

When it comes to the troubles and difficulties of life, how can we be more consciously focus on what Jesus has done for us, versus what He hasn't?

In the midst of your most painful trial, how have you seen Jesus' grace be sufficient for you? How have you seen His power made complete in your weakness?

Journal
Is there something in your life you've been spending precious energy trying to solve or figure out? If there doesn't appear to be a clear answer this side of heaven—or at least in the foreseeable future—take a moment to entrust your situation to the God who knows. Lay it before the One to whom no mysteries exist. Record a prayer in your journal.

Take Action
This is the final week of the study, so finish strong. Get in a quiet place with no distractions as you work on the homework for Session 7. Take notes and highlight anything that you might want to share with the group during the next time you meet.

- **Memorize:** 2 Corinthians 13:11
  Break the memory verse down into two or three parts to memorize. Then attempt to recite it aloud from memory to a friend or family member.

DAY 1

Spending Our Stuff and Ourselves (2 Cor. 12:11-18)

Welcome to the first day of the last week of *All Things New*! I'm seriously praising God for you. You've pressed on, and you're in the process of finishing a good work that will continue to affect lives not only here on earth, but also for eternity. My hope is that you've seen how applicable the gospel is to real life, your life. We've emphasized the message of Christ's strength in our weakness, which I hope you're experiencing as a reality and not just a concept. We've seen how Paul kept an open heart, no matter the pain, because nothing was more important than the Corinthians knowing their lives could be made totally new through Jesus—even if Paul got hurt in the process. And we're not done yet! We're headed into a very relational ending to Paul's letter. Let's finish strong!

Read 2 Corinthians 12:11-18.

I love the way verse 11 opens. What reason die Paul give for making a fool of himself?

Sometimes people just drive us to our wit's end—they test us to the ends of our patience. But when we step back from the frustration of giving to people who don't seem to get it, we realize the Lord must really love these people if He's asking us to wear ourselves out like this.

Personal Response: According to today's text, how would you sum up the main dispute the Corinthians had with Paul?

There's little that's more discouraging than when the people you help or serve tell you there's someone who they think ministers a bit better than you. After all Paul did for the Corinthians, a few of them abandoned his leadership for the Super Apostle bandwagon. This had to be heartbreaking for Paul personally, but even more troubling was how this might unravel the church.

In response to their obsession with the super apostles, Paul mentioned three proofs of his apostleship (v. 12). What were they?

As the early church emerged, validating signs, awe-inspiring wonders, and miracles that revealed God's power were proofs of the apostles' spiritual authority.

Read Acts 14:8-15.

What untimely reaction transpired in Lystra after Paul healed the lame man?

According to verse 15, what was Paul and Barnabas' goal?

Paul provided supernatural proof of his apostleship in many places, but it didn't always convince unbelieving hearts. As we can see from some of the critics in Corinth, despite what he'd shown them, some were still following after false apostles.

I believe that the Lord still works wonders and miracles today—and I'm so grateful He does—but I also believe equal, if not greater, proofs of our faith and discipleship exist.

Perhaps you've thought, *If only I could perform a miracle or throw a sign into the sky for someone, I know she'd believe.* Sometimes we wish we could prove our faith by some supernatural happening that would leave no doubt in anyone's mind about the reality of the gospel. Yet, even after Jesus performed miracles in the midst of the Jews, many of them didn't believe (John 12:37). While we may wish for a miracle to prove the gospel, I believe the way we love people and display the fruit of the Spirit are the most convincing proofs of all. Consider how effective our testimony is when we're:

1. *Content in the Lord in much or in little*
2. *Love each other selflessly*
3. *Forgive when it doesn't make sense*
4. *Trust God's sovereignty in the midst of hardship*
5. *Rejoice in the unseen realities of our hope in Christ*
6. _____. **(Fill in your own.)**

While I hope we never stop believing in God's miraculous powers, let's never forget that our love may still be the greatest proof of the gospel today.

In verses 13-14, Paul related how he went out of his way to not be a _____ to the Corinthians. Fill in the blank from this selection:

burden   imposition   inconvenience   apostle

One of the chief complaints of the Corinthians was that Paul didn't accept financial support from them. They took this to mean they were inferior to the other churches, when in reality Paul didn't want to put an added burden on them. They should have felt more loved, not less. This issue goes beyond mere support and reveals issues of control and comparison thinking.

Paul was so selfless in serving the Corinthians that I'm not sure they knew what to do with it. Sometimes we don't know what to do when someone selflessly serves us, when he or she gives without looking for something in return. This is where our pride and sense of independence can start squirming. We want to earn people's love and affection, which is really no love at all. Perhaps we're more like the Corinthian church than we think.

Not only did Paul spend his resources and himself on loving the Corinthians, he sacrificed something else very personal to him. Who did Paul send to Corinth on his behalf (vv. 17-18)?

We may not fully realize the sacrifice it was for Paul to send some of his dearest friends and ministry partners to visit Corinth. Not only would he miss their day-to-day partnership, but he also had no idea what awaited them, and he couldn't control their fate. I read a biography on the great missionary pioneer, Hudson Taylor, and was amazed at the relationships he sacrificed to bring the gospel to China. Sharing the gospel can bring great joy, but it can also bring great sacrifice, whether you're letting loved ones go so they can fulfill God's calling, or you're the one who's stepping out. Faith is required for both.

Let's consider whether we're clinging to any of our relationships too tightly. We don't want to refuse an assignment from God because we can't let go of someone. And neither do we want to hold our loved ones back from God's calling on their lives because of our selfish demands. While releasing those we cherish to follow God's leading will occasionally mean physical separation, much of the time it requires a different kind of sacrifice. It may mean a close friend sacrificing spring break to go on a mission trip, or a change of schools that may be challenging (but good) for you. Bottom line, the people we love are most blessed when we release them to the Lord. And so are we.

Personal Response: Ask the Holy Spirit to reveal to you if there's anyone you're holding too tightly. If there is, pray for the grace to release that loved one to the Lord, freeing you both up to do the work God has placed on your lives. I truly believe that our relationships are most full when they're first offered to the Lord.

DAY 2
Three Fears, One Solution (2 Cor. 12:19-21)

"I suppose that all Christian workers have found it much easier to lead people out of Egypt, than to get them into the land of Promise."[1] These words were written by Paget Wilkes, an English missionary to Japan who lived from 1871-1934. His point: It's easier to get people to leave their life of sin than to lead them into living the abundant Christian life to its full capacity. Like the Israelites, we're so glad to be free of Egypt's bondage that we settle for life in the desert. It's as if it never occurs to us that the Lord led us out of Egypt (misery of our sin) to get us into the promised land (abundant life in Jesus). Wilkes' quote reminds me of what Paul dealt with in Corinth. A brand new church had begun, people had been saved, but they were living according to their flesh, content as immature believers. Today, we'll look at what threatened them about moving into the full life Jesus came to bring.

Read 2 Corinthians 12:19-21.

As Paul prepared to make his third visit to Corinth, he mentioned four fears. The first is found in verse 20 where he said he was afraid he wouldn't find the Corinthian believers in the place of faith he hoped. (And—second—if they were in a bad place, then they wouldn't be all that excited to see him either.)

> **Personal Reflection: Describe a time when you had anxiety over seeing someone you hadn't seen in awhile. What were your worries? How did you prepare yourself? Did it go as you expected or were you surprised?**

> **Paul's third fear was finding the church filled with disobedience. Review verse 20, and list the eight sinful behaviors he feared he'd find.**

> **Personal Response: Review the list. Which one have you seen cause the most damage in the church and in your personal life, and why?**

Every time I check-in at the airport, I'm reminded of all the hazardous materials I'm not supposed to be carrying. The list is extensive, with any one of the items having the ability to cause harm or even bring the plane down, God forbid. I sort of hate being confronted with this list every time I fly, because it reminds me of all the things that could go wrong. I miss the days when peanut allergies were the big concern.

When it comes to the health of the church, the hazardous materials are not things like lithium batteries, as you well know. They're "quarreling, jealousy, outbursts of anger, selfish ambitions, slander, gossip, arrogance, and disorder" (2 Cor. 12:20, HCSB). Girls, may it not be so of us.

It's easy to read a verse like this in the way we glance through the hazardous materials list at the airport—barely paying attention, sure that none of that stuff is in our bags. But let's take a thorough and honest look at the eight destructive behaviors again, and make sure none of these are characteristic of us.

> **Personal Reflection: Review the list, asking the Holy Spirit to show you if any of these behaviors are true of you. I'm doing the same. At whatever point you're convicted, journal a confession to the Lord, remembering that He is faithful and just to forgive and purify you (1 John 1:9). Also, list any specific steps you will take to make changes.**

I'm amazed at how destructive seemingly harmless sins can be. Things like sharing negative information about someone under the veil of a prayer request, secretly wishing a person failure because you're jealous of her success, losing your temper when things don't go your way, or harboring arrogance because, after all, the way you do things is so much cooler and relevant than the other person's way. We can justify these behaviors and, at times, even dress them up to appear spiritual. However, we've just walked a weapon into the holy body that Jesus calls His church. I want us to be people who build up the body of Christ, not tear it down.

> **Paul noted his fourth fear in verse 21. What three additional sinful behaviors was he afraid he'd find the Corinthians continuing to engage in?**
> **1.**
>
> **2.**
>
> **3.**
>
>
> **All three of these are sexual in nature. Turn back to 1 Corinthians 6:18-20. Explain what is particularly destructive about sexual sin, and why it's vital to honor God with our bodies.**

Review 2 Corinthians 12:21. I want you to notice a significant concept that's easy to miss. Paul said he was afraid he'd be grieved over those who had not _____ over their sexual sin.

repented   stopped   changed   paid their dues

The word *repent* means to change one's mind for the better, to literally turn around from our sin to an obedient walk with the Lord. Romans 2:4 reminds us that God's kindness is what leads us to repentance. It's His tender hand tapping us on the shoulder, sometimes yanking us by the collar, to save us from destruction and lead us back to His life-giving side. Paul's grief wasn't over the Corinthians' past sexual sins for which they already repented and received forgiveness. He was troubled over the previous pattern of sexual sin some Corinthians persisted in. There's a difference.

While dealing with our sins can be an unpleasant task, it's necessary. Repentance is required to experience the full life Jesus longs to give us. We simply can't have His abundant life while hanging onto our sexual addictions, gossip, hatred, unforgiveness, or whatever sin we're clutching. Even though Paul had three pressing fears concerning the harmful behaviors of the Corinthians, he started today's passage with an indisputable positive. Look back at verse 19.

What endearing term did Paul use to refer to the Corinthians?

What motivated Paul to do the things he did for them?

Paul and his friends challenged the people they loved in Corinth, because they considered them dear friends. Many were brothers and sisters in Christ. They persisted in their ministry because they wanted the Corinthians to be built up, edified, and strengthened. They didn't minister according to their own rules or decision-making skills but in the sight of God, as people who lived in the love and boundaries of Christ and His character.

If you're sensing the conviction of the Spirit in regard to any of the sins we've discussed today, I pray you'll sense God's kindness all over His conviction. I pray you'll see that turning from the harmful sins that wound others and yourself is for the sole purpose of turning to the abundant life Jesus has come to offer. Take absolutely whatever step is necessary to confess, repent, and free yourself from any sins you're participating in. Jesus has already finished the work of making a way for your purity; you need only to take Him up on it.

so when you, a mere human being, pass judgment on them and yet do the same things, do you think you will escape God's judgment? Or do you show contempt for the riches of his kindness, forbearance and patience, not realizing that God's kindness is intended to lead you to repentance?
Romans 2:3—4

DAY 3
The Proof of Christ *(2 Cor. 13:1-4)*

The final chapter of Paul's letter opened with a word about his upcoming third visit to the Corinthians. To refresh your memory, Paul visited Corinth for the first time in A.D. 50 and stayed for one and a half years. His second visit was what many refer to as the "painful visit," which was mentioned in 2 Corinthians 2:1-2. It was painful because Paul found the young church fallen into the strong sway of materialism, immorality, and false beliefs that were popular at the time. As Paul continued to prepare the church for his third visit, he desperately hoped to find them in good standing with himself and, more importantly, with the Lord.

Read 2 Corinthians 13:1-4

Paul came out swinging here. You may be wondering if his love had run out, if he finally reached the bottom of his mercy and grace barrel. Remember Paul was constantly patient. He spared them, pleaded with them, performed miracles among them, wrote to them, sent his best friends their way, and visited them personally. He even took an Old Testament mandate to extra lengths to make sure he didn't act hastily or in error.

Jot down the Old Testament law Paul quoted in verse 1, originally given in Deuteronomy 19:15.

In ancient Israelite culture, when someone was accused of committing a sin, the accusation had to be validated by two or more witnesses. This helped confirm the facts and safeguard anyone from being falsely accused or wrongly punished. I believe Paul used this passage metaphorically, meaning that his previous two visits, two warnings, and upcoming visit would serve as the 2-3 witnesses needed to establish a conviction. In other words, Paul had been as thorough, patient, and measured as possible, but it was time to deal with the sin that harmed the church.

Unlike Paul, sometimes I'm guilty of judging someone based only on rumors. Other times I'm guilty of not confronting a person who I know is living in a destructive pattern of sin.

Personal Reflection: How does Paul's balance of patiently investigating the problems in Corinth and his willingness to decisively deal with those problems challenge you? In other words, how can you be slower to judge when you don't know all the facts, yet quicker to lovingly confront when you do?

When I look at today's verses I see one word at the heart of the chaos and conflict in Corinth. What can it all be boiled down to (v. 2)?

When my niece Maryn was six years old, she had this great conversation with my sister Katie on the way home from Sunday school. "Mom," she asked from the backseat of the car, "What is sin?"

"Well, it's that thing we've talked about when you don't share with your brother, or you talk back to Mommy and Daddy," Katie said while maneuvering traffic. "Sometimes, when you know you've done something wrong, you have that bad feeling we've talked about."

"Oh yeah, I remember now," Maryn affirmed. Like, she had this sin thing down. A couple hours went by and Katie had all but forgotten the conversation when Maryn approached her with all her Italian hand gestures (my sister married a New Jersey Italian), "Mom, Judah ran his big wheel into my tricycle today just to be mean." Pausing a second, she emphatically continued, "I mean, talk about *sin*!"

I second Maryn's sentiments—talk about some sin in Corinth! Some of the Corinthians had reveled in it and drew others into it with them. Sin, it's the ruthless thing we deal with. It's the thing that ruins relationships, dissolves trust, fuels jealousy, stirs selfishness, harbors unforgiveness, and fractures goodness. Praise God, He has made a way for us to escape its vicious tendrils.

In verses 3-4, Paul mentioned the crucifixion and resurrection of Jesus, His weakness and His power. Paul brought this up because a few of the ungodly leaders in Corinth apparently questioned whether Jesus truly spoke through Paul. Paul's response was that Jesus was surely powerful among them and would not be weak in dealing with them. Recently, I've been mindful of the Lord's gracious dealings with me in times of wandering and disobedience. I wasn't particularly grateful for the discipline at the time, but looking back I'm so thankful He was powerful in rescuing me from my sin.

Look back at verse 3. What did the Corinthians demand from Paul?

I've been thinking a lot lately about what the proof of Jesus' activity in our lives looks like. The other day, I ran into someone at the store I hadn't seen in a while. He's had a lot of success in Christian media and just landed another huge deal. One of the things he said was, "I'm just really enjoying God's favor right now." Please hear me say I'm not judging God's favor on a person's life—this large deal could very well be part of God's blessing on my acquaintance. But it gave me pause. Is the proof of Jesus' hand on our lives found only in money, flashes of fame, and our biggest dreams coming true? Or is the proof of His power also found in us when we are given grace to love the unlovely, forgive when it flies in the face of our gut reaction, and hear His Holy Spirit whisper tender words of encouragement to our broken hearts?

The church at Corinth still looked for Paul to come with showy signs and gushing expressions of power, maybe even wealth. I think we sometimes look for the same types of things in our lives to decide if Jesus is really present in us—or in someone else. Again, we see Paul bring a mystery back around that I hope we'll never forget: Christ reigned by God's power, and He was crucified in weakness. In the same way, Paul had several areas of weakness in his life, yet God's power was extraordinarily strong in Him.

I truly don't believe Paul advocated for a brand of Christianity where everyone is incompetent, unskilled, and dead broke because we're trying to avoid anything that looks like strength or success. That is not what it means to be weak in Christ. What it does mean is that in the areas where we are truly weak, we can rely on the power of God to work in our weakness. And where we are strong in this world, we offer that strength to God as if it were weakness because even our greatest strength is not as strong as the weakness of God (1 Cor. 1:25). Our skills, accomplishments, and possessions, while good things, cannot be the sole proof of His favor on our lives. What Paul expressed in Philippians 3 is that none of our strengths compare to knowing Christ.

Dear friend, make sure you're not judging the proof of God's hand on your life merely by outward, materialistic blessings. These certainly can be part of His favor, make no mistake. But as we've seen throughout 2 Corinthians, oftentimes His greatest display of power in our lives is in our places of loneliness, battles with sickness, and painful losses. Whether you're feeling weak or strong, hide yourself as weak in Christ, as a child is weak when resting in her father's arms. This is where we'll find the true strength to love God and serve others.

DAY 4
Passing The Test *(2 Cor. 13:5-10)*

Read 2 Corinthians 13:5-10 thoughtfully.

> **Focus for a moment on verse 5. What are your thoughts and responses as you consider this verse?**

Verses like 13:5 used to throw me into a tailspin of fear and uncertainty. *Have I passed the test? Am I really a true Christian? What if I've been disqualified, and I don't know it? How can I know if Jesus is really in me?* If these troubling thoughts haven't already crossed your mind, I'm glad I've now made you aware. I wish I'd known at the time that Paul meant this to be an affirming question, carrying the idea of "proving in the expectation of approving."[2] In other words, Paul wanted the Corinthians to take a hard look at themselves with the expectation that they would discover Jesus Christ was truly in their lives and working in their midst. As a result, they would also see Paul as an authentic minister of Christ and would orient their lives around the truth He taught them.

The reason for examining and testing is to discover the true nature or character of something, to determine its genuineness.[3] So when Paul talked about testing and examining yourself, he spoke in terms of a person being qualified as a true believer. The hopeful expectation is that a person is tested and found to have a genuine faith.

It would be as if your math teacher, right before passing out final exams said, "Class, don't you realize how smart and accomplished you are? You've applied yourselves all year! I want you to take this test because it's going to prove to you everything you've learned. I have no doubt you'll succeed." You would receive this as encouragement and inspiration, making you eager to take the test. The positive test result would more substantially prove what was already there.

While Paul's desire was for the Corinthians to examine themselves to affirm Jesus Christ was truly in their midst, he couldn't possibly know the spiritual state of every person who'd hear his letter. Thus the phrase, "unless you fail the test." Meaning, there might be a few who would examine themselves and realize they'd never come into relationship with Jesus, they'd never looked to Him to cleanse them of their sins, and had no desire to live according to Paul's apostolic teaching. If you're concerned about whether or not you're in the faith, the good news of the gospel is that in order to pass the test, you simply have to trust in the Savior who passed it for you. We'll get to this at the close of today's study.

Read verses 6-7 again. What did Paul hope the Corinthians would finally discover about him and his fellow ministers?

I find verse 7 convicting. Paul desperately hoped the Corinthians would stop sinning so they could do what was right, but not for the ultimate purpose of him looking good. If they didn't shape up, then he would have the opportunity to really show off his spiritual authority. But he was far more concerned about their spiritual health than his reputation. He would rather they repent on their own so he could visit them as a gentler Paul, instead of as an authority who only disciplined them.

Personal Reflection: Is there anyone in your life you hope will get his or her act together more for your sake than for theirs? Ask the Lord to purify your motives in this relationship.

As we disciple and come alongside others it's important for us to evaluate our heart's motives. I've often wanted the people around me to align their Christian beliefs closer to mine or clean up their behavior more for my benefit and reputation than out of genuine concern for their relationship with Christ. Sometimes, I want to help people because I'll come off looking extra wise and spiritual. At other times my biggest concern is having people on my theological side. For Paul, even if he looked like a failure he didn't care. He just wanted the people he loved so dearly to stop their destructive behavior, so they could live righteously for Jesus. My hope is that I'm becoming more like this, with my priority to grow up others in the Lord, regardless of my reputation.

Review verse 8 and fill in the blank. Whether Paul found the Corinthians in blatant sin or in humble repentance, when he arrived he'd act according to the _____.

Personal Response: Review verses 9-10. What do you think Paul meant when he said he was happy when he was weak and the Corinthians were strong?

Growing up with my parents in ministry meant seeing some difficult confrontations over the years. Neither one of my parents took joy in slinging their ministerial authority around or coming off as large and in charge. I know my Dad would rather humbly teach and shepherd his people as they served the Lord versus having to authoritatively confront those who were causing division. In similar fashion, Paul's desire for the Corinthians to be restored trumped his concern for how they viewed him. He would much prefer the people perceive him as weak, rather than having to show off his authoritative strength. He wanted to come with gentle authority to build them up, not tear them down.

I hope the Lord is piercing your heart for people and their spiritual growth. My desire is that He's convicting you to show grace before punishment, to give the benefit of the doubt before judgment, and to see the good of others as superior to your personal gain. I also hope that if you hesitate to stand up for what's right or confront someone who's in sin, you'll find courage to step up if need be. However you're led to use your authority, remember it's given by God and for building others up. Keep in mind that this will look different in different situations.

I want to close by going back to verse 5. There, Paul challenged the Corinthians to examine themselves to make sure they were true believers. He made this request with the optimistic expectation that they'd realize anew Jesus Christ was in them.

While I believe many of the original hearers of the letter were found confident in their faith, I also believe some who heard this question needed to go to Jesus Christ and receive Him as Savior. Maybe the same is true today. If you don't know Christ, nothing would make me happier than to know you placed your faith in Jesus today and received Him as your Savior. And if you're already a believer, what joyful affirmation to once again recognize Jesus in your midst.

Read what Paul said in Acts 13:38-39. It is also listed in the margin.

Yesterday I went to my mailbox and pulled out a letter from a 12-year-old boy named Daniel who goes to my parent's church. Daniel was born with a brain tumor and has recently gone blind as a result. The letter was written in Braille. He wrote to thank me for singing "Happy Birthday" to him the week before. Here are his precious and poignant words:

"Kelly, Thank you for singing to me. Do you know Jesus? Love, Daniel."

Paul asked the Corinthians. Daniel asked me. And today I have asked you: Do you know Jesus?

"Therefore, my friends, I want you to know that through Jesus the forgiveness of sins is proclaimed to you. Through him everyone who believes is set free from every sin, a justification you were not able to obtain under the law of Moses."
Acts 13:38-39

DAY 5
Grace, Love & Fellowship *(2 Cor. 13:11-14)*

A lot of life has happened since I first gave myself to studying and teaching 2 Corinthians. You know how that goes. We have our jobs, the daily mundane activities, perhaps a trying hardship, along with some really joyous occasions and celebratory milestones. It's in the midst of all this life that what I really believe about the truths of 2 Corinthians has been tested. Truths such as God's comfort in pain, His power through the weak vessel of my being, Christ's sufficient grace in enduring trials. *Will I love people with my heart stretched a little wider, even the difficult ones? Do I consider giving a burden or a tremendous privilege? Am I serving others with the power and life of new covenant ministry?*

As we come to the end of a journey, I want to finish by returning to where we started. 2 Corinthians was written to real people, in a real city, because the gospel is meant to thrive in real life. My prayer is that what we've learned along the way will not be mere knowledge, but will be put into practice in our lives. I don't think Paul would have written 2 Corinthians for anything less than for the church to live it. For us to live it.

As we finish our final day of homework together let's read Paul's closing words to the Corinthian church.

Read 2 Corinthians 13:11-14

> **Paul left the Corinthians with 5 commands in verse 11. Because translations vary, I've included the HCSB translation in the margin for you to work from.**
>
> 1.   *Rejoice (farewell or goodbye)*
> 2.
> 3.
> 4.
> 5.
>
> **Personal Response: Knowing the difficulties in the Corinthian church, which of the five commands do you think would be the most challenging for them and why?**

After Paul's first directive to "rejoice," he called them to "become mature," or to reach for restoration. The community of believers in Corinth had settled for something short of the fullness of

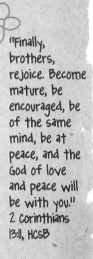

"Finally, brothers, rejoice. Become mature, be encouraged, be of the same mind, be at peace, and the God of love and peace will be with you."
2 Corinthians 13:11, HCSB

restoration to God. This simple phrase is more meaningful than we may give it credit for. Paul pushed them to keep pressing toward spiritual maturity and be equipped and fitted for ministry. Just this morning, I confessed to the Lord how easily satisfied I can be with status quo Christianity, both individually and within my community of believers. I may try to get by with a quick quiet time with the Lord, church attendance, time with friends throughout the week and some entertainment here or there. I can settle for being out of the pit of sin, but not fully in a place of thriving spiritual maturity. But we see in verse 11 we're to press, aim, reach to become spiritually grown-up—especially within our churches and believing communities. I really believe one of the messages Paul wanted to get across is "Don't settle!"

How does Paul's third command relate to 2 Corinthians 1:3-7? Describe different ways we can put this into practice.

I find the fourth directive to be a little tricky. I would wholeheartedly love to be of one mind with everyone. Of course, as long as they all agreed with me. But this is rarely the case, as you well know.

Personal Response: What are some possible characteristics of a body of believers that is of one mind, or in agreement with one another?

Being of one mind doesn't necessarily mean we all agree on every point of the Christian faith. Now, we should always agree on the essentials, holding to the fundamentals of the faith, such as the death and resurrection of Jesus, the Trinity, and salvation being found in Him and Him alone. While there may be room for disagreement over secondary issues, our fellowship together must always be characterized by Christian virtues, such as humility, kindness, gentleness, compassion, patience, and so on. We may have differing opinions on some important issues, but we must always strive to have in common the non-negotiable abiding fruit of the Spirit. Above all, we should put on love.

What is the result of living out these 5 instructions, according to the end of verse 11?

Paul's second to last thoughts revolved around the warmth of community unique to the family of Christ: "greet one another with a holy kiss," and all the saints send their greetings. While greeting one another with kisses was common to both Jews and Greeks at the time, the holy kiss seemed to originate with Paul. It signaled the affection found in a family that opened its arms wide to any person from any race, culture, or background who names Christ as Savior. No family on earth is as diverse or welcoming as the family of Christ.

Paul extended confidence and grace, letting the Corinthians know that all the saints (most likely the Macedonians) send their greetings. Even though the Corinthian church had struggled, Paul counted them among the saints, worthy to receive the Macedonian church's warm affection. This gracious closing shows Paul still saw the Corinthians as true brothers and sisters in the Lord, despite the pain and difficult relationships. He still considered them family.

I can't think of a better ending to 2 Corinthians than the way Paul closed this letter.

Draw a line between each member of the Trinity and the corresponding blessing Paul mentions.

Jesus   Grace

God   Fellowship

Holy Spirit   Love

Nowhere else did Paul leave such a strong picture of the Trinity. Despite the problems in Corinth, no division of pain or hardship could overcome the grace, love, and fellowship of Jesus Christ, God the Father, and the Holy Spirit. Paul didn't end the letter by focusing on himself, because he knew that he was not the answer the church needed. His only hope for the church at Corinth was the same hope to which we cling today: the grace of Jesus.

I want to echo Paul's prayer as we cross the finish line of this study.

May the grace of Jesus meet you at every step, may you be bundled in the love of God, and may the Holy Spirit commune with you in places no human can reach. And if I may borrow from an earlier portion of Paul's letter, whenever you are weak may you find Christ in you as gloriously strong. For since His coming, the old order of powerlessness in sin and brokenness is passed away, behold all things have been made new.

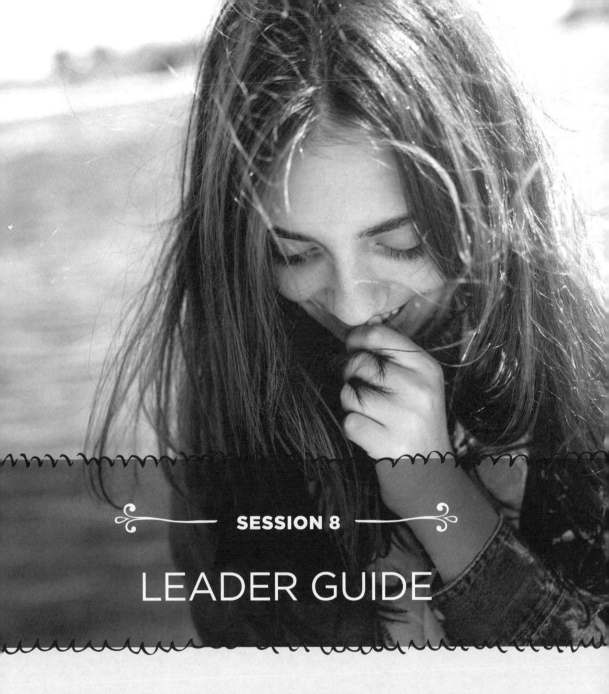

LEADER GUIDE

Way to go! Thank you for pressing on and sticking with this study until the end. This final session is where you'll find all of the Leader Guide information, as well as a Group Guide covering the last week of homework from Session 7.

As you have journeyed through one of Paul's most personal letters in the homework and during group time, our prayer is that you've learned about Christ's power in our weaknesses, generosity, the new covenant we have in Christ Jesus, and how He makes *all things new*!

Group Guide (Week 8)

Prepare

Spend some time praying for your group leader, as well as for your pastor and those on staff at your church. Thank God for them and how He has used them in your life. Be still, and take some time to reflect on God's faithfulness in your own life.

Review & Discuss

Flip back through your homework from Session 7, and highlight anything that was significant to you or that you want share with others.

Then, spend some time discussing the homework from Session 7.

Turn to the following references and note what characteristics show the world we're disciples of Jesus.

• John 13:34-35

• Galatians 5:22

In Day 1's homework, you learned how the Corinthians had issues with control and comparison thinking. Consider the following questions based on your study from Day 1:

Control: The Corinthians wanted Paul to receive financial support from them. As we touched on earlier, how might this be used to control him?

Comparison Thinking: According to verse 13, how did the Corinthians believe they compared to other churches based on the fact Paul had received support from those churches?

What single thing from 2 Corinthians has challenged you the most?

Have you ever considered that your weaknesses could actually be proof of Christ's hand on your life, because He wants to show Himself strong in those areas? Explain.

After completing this study, how can you and your group help the church community you're a part of keep from settling spiritually?

What are two significant takeaways you have from 2 Corinthians?

Journal

How has Jesus specifically shown His power in dealing with sin or temptation in your life? After you write a brief description, spend some time thanking Him for His active power working in your life.

Take Action

Look back through your notes and what you have learned over the last seven weeks. Share what God has taught you with a family member or friend, or even consider helping to lead a younger group of girls through this study. Ask God to help you apply what you've learned. Pray for the other girls in your group, and continue to keep them accountable to living in light of the new covenant and as new creations in Christ.

- **Memorize:** 2 Corinthians 5:17
  You've likely already memorized this verse, but if not, commit it to memory. Make a lock-screen for your phone with this verse displayed so you'll have a reminder from this study in 2 Corinthians, even in the weeks and months to come.

LEADER GUIDE

session 1 (Week 1)
The Church in the City *(2 Cor. 1:1–2:11)*

Prepare
As you prepare to meet with girls, spend some time praying for them. Pray that this study would draw them closer to the Lord and give them a deeper understanding of His Word.

Consider the room or location in which you will meet and try to make it as comfortable for girls as possible. Think about providing some drinks and snacks, depending on the time you meet. If most of the girls do not know each other, you might want to consider beginning your time with an ice breaker or get-to-know-you activity.

Review & Discuss
Spend some time introducing yourself, as well as the study and the context of 2 Corinthians. Read the introduction together as a group, and then discuss the questions included in the Group Guide on pages 12-13.

In the Group Guide, girls were asked to list one thing they learned, as well as one question they have. Be prepared if they ask you. If you do not have an answer, that's alright. Just let her know you will research it and get back with her later.

Take Action
Emphasize the importance of the girls keeping each other accountable. The first few weeks tend to be easier, but encourage them to press on and not get discouraged if they get behind on the readings and homework for Session 2. Send a text three or four days prior to your next meeting as a reminder about your next Bible study group meeting.

- **Memorize:** 2 Corinthians 1:5-6
  Encourage girls sometime during the week by sharing 2 Corinthians 1:5-6 with them. Commit it to memory yourself this week.

session 2 (Week 2)
The God of All Comfort *(2 Cor. 2:12–4:18)*

Prepare
You may have a few new girls who missed the first week, so be prepared to introduce them to the group and catch them up on what they missed from Session 1.

Review & Discuss

As you review and prepare to meet and discuss the homework from Session 1 in 2 Corinthians 1:1—2:11, you'll address sincerity and suffering. Both are somewhat weighty topics, so be mindful of that and understand that some girls may be facing trials or suffering. Pray that this will be a beneficial time for all in your group, and ask God to give you wisdom and discernment as you help to guide the conversation.

You've already talked some about the context of 2 Corinthians, but take a few minutes to recap what the church at Corinth was probably like and the importance of knowing where, when, and to whom this book of the Bible was written (Day 1). Then discuss the questions included in the Group Guide on pages 32-33. Be sensitive and understanding as you address the subject of suffering, and guide discussion back to Scripture while emphasizing the benefits of suffering that we often tend to overlook.

Ask several girls to share what they learned about themselves from the *How Sincere Am I?* quiz.

Then, challenge girls to be sincere in their relationships, to confess their sins, and ask God to cleanse their consciences if they have any insincerity in their hearts. Let them know that their homework for this week will build on last week's as they learn how God comforts us and gives us the hope of heaven (2 Cor. 4:14).

Take Action

If your group is interested, schedule an opportunity to serve those who might be suffering. Be open to their ideas. You might start by contacting your church's senior adult ministry to see where there are needs, or find a way girls can send notes of encouragement to the homebound or minister to those at a local nursing home.

- **Memorize:** 2 Corinthians 4:17

Session 3 (Week 3)
A New Ministry *(2 Cor. 5:1–7:1)*

Prepare

Ask God to use your weaknesses for His glory and to give you confidence in Him, not in things of this earth. Pray for the girls in your group, specifically that they would continually fix their eyes on Jesus. Review what you studied and learned in Session 2, and then read the introduction to Session 3. Take notes and highlight important points.

Review & Discuss

If you would like to take a different approach to your group time, one way to do this is to spend 5-10 minutes in silence as you each read through the following questions and journal your answers. Then, share your responses with the entire group, or form smaller groups of 2-3 to share with.

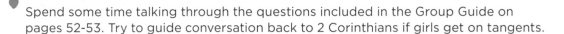

Spend some time talking through the questions included in the Group Guide on pages 52-53. Try to guide conversation back to 2 Corinthians if girls get on tangents.

Take Action

Kelly said we are called to rejoice that the light of Christ is most brilliant in our weaknesses. In what ways do you need to rejoice in your weaknesses this week?

Consider whether you are distancing yourself from serving God in a way that requires commitment. If so, why? Spend time confessing this to the Lord and asking for courage to change directions.

- **Memorize:** 2 Corinthians 5:21
  Encourage girls to commit to memorize this verse. Provide some time for girls to creatively display this verse on a canvas or whatever they want to paint it on. Suggest they bring their canvas or surface, and you can provide the paints. Consider playing "Jesus Messiah" (*Passion: Awakening [Deluxe Edition]*, Sparrow, 2010) by Chris Tomlin during this time as the lyrics to this song are from 2 Corinthians 5:21.

Session 4 (Week 4)
The New has Come (*2 Cor. 7:2–8:24*)

Prepare

Re-read 2 Corinthians 5:1–7:1, review your notes from the week, and then read the introduction for Session 4. Pray for your girls as you approach this session on giving. Ask God to make you generous and that He would prepare the hearts of each of the girls as they continue to read and study 2 Corinthians.

Review & Discuss

As a group, read through and discuss the questions included in the Group Guide on pages 72-73. To prevent one person from dominating the conversation, you might choose to go around in a circle, and give girls a brief opportunity to share their thoughts and answers.

Take Action

It's easy to send out a group text or email, but try to be intentional to reach out to girls individually.

- **Memorize:** 2 Corinthians 8:9
  Read this verse aloud. Then, ask the girls in your group what the grace of Jesus means to them. Remind them if they know Jesus, they have the greatest gift they could possibly have and they are rich in Him.

Session 5 (Week 5)
Rethinking Generosity (*2 Cor. 9:1–10:18*)

Prepare

Pray for the endurance to continue on strong in this Bible study. Review your homework and any notes from the last session, and read the introduction for Session 5, as well as 2 Corinthians 9:1–10:18.

Review & Discuss
Use the Group Guide on pages 92-93 for help with conversation starters and a guide for discussion regarding the reading for the week in 2 Corinthians. Give girls the opportunity to ask any questions they might have. Encourage them to take notes so that they are able to go back and reference what your group has discussed at a later date.

Take Action
In this session's Group Guide, girls were guided write a note of encouragement. Be sure they have stamps and everything they need to complete this during the week.

Continue to review and recap what girls have already studied and learned in 2 Corinthians each week at the beginning of your group time, and consider posting a brief summary/review on social media for those who might have missed the session. Contact them to let them know they were missed and that you hope to see them back for the next group meeting.

- **Memorize:** 2 Corinthians 9:6

session 6 (week 6)
The Tide *(2 Cor. 11:1–12:10)*

Prepare
If some girls in your group are more musically inclined, you might consider asking them to lead you in worship at the start of your group session one week. Ask them what they might need so you can help facilitate for this time of worship.

Review & Discuss
Talk through the Group Guide questions on pages 112-113 and give girls an opportunity to share their thoughts.

Take Action
Pray for friends and family who do not know Jesus. Guide girls to share and list some ways they can help point their friends and family to Christ.

- **Memorize:** 2 Corinthians 12:9

session 7 (week 7)
All Things New *(2 Cor. 12:11–13:14)*

Prepare
Look back on your notes and try to prepare a recap and broad overview of the themes you've studied throughout your time in 2 Corinthians.

Review & Discuss

Read and review Session 7 and the homework, highlighting what you want to discuss more in depth with your group. We've provided the Group Guide questions on pages 132-133 as a starting point for discussion. Give girls the opportunity to share their thoughts and what they've gained as a whole from this study.

As you discuss the personal relationship evaluation on page 132 with your group, emphasize that our hearts need to be purified and Christ needs to be first. If conversation drifts, steer the group back and move on to the next question.

After you read Galatians 5:6-12, remind girls to go to Scripture and compare what they are hearing others say—even their pastor—to what God's Word says.

Take Action

Encourage girls to memorize the following verse by memorizing it with them.

• **Memorize:** 2 Corinthians 13:11

Session 8 (Week 8)
Closing

Prepare

Consider bringing a snack or doing something special for your group. This could be any sort of small token to remind them of 2 Corinthians, or write each girl a personalized note if you have time.

Review & Discuss

As you conclude your study of 2 Corinthians, use the Group Guide questions on pages 151-152 to help guide the group discussion. Allow time for girls to share and discuss, but try to keep the conversation as focused on 2 Corinthians as possible.

Take Action

Make an effort to pray for and keep in touch with the girls in your group even after this study has ended. That might mean sending a quick text, meeting for coffee, or writing them notes to let them know you're praying for them.

• **Memorize:** 2 Corinthians 5:17

SOURCES

Session 1

1. Ralph P. Martin, *Word Biblical Commentary, Volume 40: 2 Corinthians* (Dallas: Word Books, 1986), xxix.
2. "Holiness," *Vines Expository Dictionary of New Testament Words*, BlueletterBible.org, accessed September 16, 2016, https://www.blueletterbible.org/search/Dictionary/viewTopic.cfm?topic=VT0001394.
3. Joseph Thayer, *Thayer's Greek-English Lexicon* (Peabody: Hendrickson Publishers, 1995).
4. W. E. Vine, *Vine's Expository Dictionary of Old and New Testament Words* (Nashville: Thomas Nelson, 1997), 733.
5. George H. Guthrie, *Baker Exegetical Commentary on the New Testament: 2 Corinthians* (Ada: Baker Academic, 2015), 102.

Session 2

1. George H. Guthrie, *Baker Exegetical Commentary on the New Testament: 2 Corinthians* (Ada: Baker Academic, 2015), 167.
2. Ibid., 206.
3. W. E. Vine, *Vine's Expository Dictionary of New Testament Words* (Zeeland: Reformed Church Publications, 2015), 247.
4. George H. Guthrie, *Baker Exegetical Commentary on the New Testament: 2 Corinthians* (Ada: Baker Academic, 2015), 269-271.

Session 3

1. C. S. Lewis, *The Weight of Glory: And Other Addresses* (New York: Harper Collins, 1980), 26.
2. "Lexicon: Strong's G4912 – synecho," *Blue Letter Bible*, accessed August 26, 2016, https://www.blueletterbible.org/lang/lexicon/lexicon.cfm?Strongs=G4912&t=NIV.
3. Eugene Peterson, *Tell It Slant: A Conversation on the Language of Jesus in His Stories and Prayers* (Grand Rapids: William B. Eerdmans Publishing, 2008), 21.
4. C. K. Barrett, *The Second Epistle to the Corinthians (Black's New Testament Commentaries)* (Grand Rapids: Baker Academic, 1993), 163, quoted in George H. Guthrie, *Baker Exegetical Commentary on the New Testament: 2 Corinthians* (Ada: Baker Academic, 2015), 293.
5. "Lexicon: Strong's G2644 – *katallasso*," *Blue Letter Bible*, accessed August 26, 2016, https://www.blueletterbible.org/lang/lexicon/lexicon.cfm?Strongs=G2644&t=NIV.
6. George H. Guthrie, *Baker Exegetical Commentary on the New Testament: 2 Corinthians* (Ada: Baker Academic, 2015), 309.
7. Ibid., 329. (emphasis mine)
8. yoke, *Merriam-Webster*, 2016. Available online at http://www.merriam-webster.com/dictionary yoke.

Session 4

1. George H. Guthrie, *Baker Exegetical Commentary on the New Testament: 2 Corinthians* (Ada: Baker Academic, 2015), 363.
2. Walter Bauer, *A Greek-English Lexicon of the New Testament and Other Early Christian Literature, 3rd ed.*, ed. Frederick W. Danker (Chicago: The University of Chicago Press, 2000), 163, quoted in George H. Guthrie, *Baker Exegetical Commentary on the New Testament: 2 Corinthians* (Ada: Baker Academic, 2015), 375.

Session 5

1. R. H. Strachan, The Second Epistle of Paul to the Corinthians (New York: Harper & Brothers, 1935), 124, quoted in Ralph P. Martin, Word Biblical Commentary: 2 Corinthians, vol. 40 (Dallas: Word, 1986), 306.
2. Philip E. Hughes, *Paul's Second Epistle to the Corinthians: The English Text with Introduction, Exposition, and Notes, New International Commentary on the New Testament* (Grand Rapids, Eerdmans, 1962), quoted in George H. Guthrie, *Baker Exegetical Commentary on the New Testament: 2 Corinthians* (Ada: Baker Academic, 2015), 436.
3. M. J. Harris, *The Second Epistle to the Corinthians: A Commentary on the Greek Text, New International Greek New Testament Commentary* (Grand Rapids: Eerdmans, 2005), 677, quoted in George H. Guthrie, *Baker Exegetical Commentary on the New Testament: 2 Corinthians* (Ada: Baker Academic, 2015), 472.
4. George H. Guthrie, *Baker Exegetical Commentary on the New Testament: 2 Corinthians* (Ada: Baker Academic, 2015), 475.
5. Ibid., 474.
6. Ralph P. Martin, *Word Biblical Commentary: 2 Corinthians, vol. 40* (Dallas: Word, 1986), 306.
7. "Gentleness," *Vines Expository Dictionary of New Testament Words*, BlueletterBible.org, accessed September 8, 2016, https://www.blueletterbible.org/search/Dictionary/viewTopic.cfm?topic=VT0001187.
8. "Gracious," *Vines Expository Dictionary of New Testament Words*, BlueletterBible.org, accessed September 8, 2016, https://www.blueletterbible.org/search/Dictionary/viewTopic.cfm?topic=VT0001231#vineDiv.
9. Matthew Arnold, *Literature & Dogma: An Essay Towards A Better Apprehension of the Bible,* (New York: McMillan and Co., 1883), 343, quoted in "Gracious," *Vines Expository Dictionary of New Testament Words,* BlueletterBible.org, accessed September 8, 2016, https://www.blueletterbible.org/search/Dictionary/viewTopic.cfm?topic=VT0001231#vineDiv.
10. George H. Guthrie, *Baker Exegetical Commentary on the New Testament: 2 Corinthians* (Ada: Baker Academic, 2015), 467.
11. "Meekness," *Vines Expository Dictionary of New Testament Words,* BlueletterBible.org, accessed September 8, 2016, https://www.blueletterbible.org/search/Dictionary/viewTopic.cfm?topic=VT0001785.

Session 6

1. Martin H. Manser, Alister E. McGrath, J. I. Packer, and Donald J. Wiseman, *Dictionary of Bible Themes: The Accessible and Comprehensive Tool for Topical Studies* (Grand Rapids: Zondervan, 1999), accessed via *mywsb.com*.
2. Timothy B. Savage, *Power Through Weakness: Paul's Understanding of the Christian Ministry in 2 Corinthians* (New York: Cambridge University Press, 1996), 87.
3. George H. Guthrie, *Baker Exegetical Commentary on the New Testament: 2 Corinthians* (Ada: Baker Academic, 2015), 583.
4. Ibid., 587.
5. Ralph P. Martin, *Word Biblical Commentary: 2 Corinthians, vol. 40* (Dallas: Word, 1986), 412.

Session 7

1. A. Paget Wilkes, *Sanctification, 13th ed.* (London: Japan Evangelistic Band), accessed September 12, 2016, http://www.enterhisrest.org/entry_directions/sanctification_w.pdf.
2. Alfred Plummer, *A Critical and Exegetical Commentary on the Second Epistle of Saint Paul to the Corinthians (International Critical Commentary Ser.) 2nd ed.* (Edinburgh: T. & T. Clark, 1915), 376, quoted in Ralph P. Martin, *Word Biblical Commentary: 2 Corinthians, vol. 40* (Dallas: Word, 1986), 478.
3. George H. Guthrie, *Baker Exegetical Commentary on the New Testament: 2 Corinthians* (Ada: Baker Academic, 2015), 638.

CHALLENGE GIRLS TO LIVE AS WORTHY VESSELS OF THE GOSPEL OF JESUS CHRIST.

A Study of 2 Timothy for Teen Girls

worthy vessel

AMY BYRD

LifeWay | Girls

Worthy Vessel is a six-session resource by Amy Byrd that will lead girls through an in-depth study of 2 Timothy. They will examine biblical context and a multitude of spiritual truths in this letter from the apostle Paul to Timothy. As they explore the relationship between Paul and his young disciple, girls will be challenged to live as worthy vessels of the gospel of Jesus Christ, encouraging others to walk in faith as they deliver the message God has entrusted to them.

AVAILABLE AT LIFEWAY.COM/GIRLS OR AT YOUR LOCAL LIFEWAY CHRISTIAN STORE.

WILL YOU JOIN
Kelly Minter

IN CARING FOR THE POOR, THE ORPHANED & FORGOTTEN?

JUSTICE & MERCY INTERNATIONAL IS A NON-PROFIT, CHRIST-CENTERED ORGANIZATION THAT CARES FOR THE VULNERABLE AND FORGOTTEN IN THE AMAZON AND MOLDOVA.

FIND OUT HOW YOU CAN HELP BY VISITING
WWW.JUSTICEANDMERCY.ORG

Justice & mercy
INTERNATIONAL